AMYRAUT

on

Predestination

THE FIRST PUBLISHED TRANSLATION FROM THE FRENCH

by

DR MATTHEW HARDING

With a Biographical Outline

by

DR ALAN C. CLIFFORD

CHARENTON REFORMED PUBLISHING

2017

Text © The Publisher 2017

Layout © Quinta Press 2017

First published in Great Britain 2017
by Charenton Reformed Publishing
www.christiancharenton.co.uk

All rights reserved

ISBN 978–0–9929465–5–5 (paperback)

ISBN 978–0–9929465–6–2 (hardback)

Typeset in Bembo 12 on 14 point
by Quinta Press, Weston Rhyn, Oswestry, Shropshire

Printed and bound in Great Britain by Lightning Source

British Library Cataloguing in Publication Data.

A catalogue record for this book is available from the British Library.

Cover concept: A. C. Clifford, formatting by Barkers Print & Design, Attleborough, Norfolk. Engraving of Amyraut courtesy of Société de l' Histoire du Protestantisme Française, Paris.

Dedicated to my loving family who has given me the time and space to follow my love of Historical Theology, French, the Reformation, and where those roads intertwine.

Contents

Introduction	7
Biographical Outline	11
Translation Theory & Technique	41
The Text	43
Amyraut's Marginalia	47
Explanatory Notes	48
Conclusion	49
Amyraut's *Brief Treatise on Predestination*	51
Table of Contents	55
Chapter 1	57
Chapter 2	63
Chapter 3	69
Chapter 4	73
Chapter 5	83
Chapter 6	91
Chapter 7	99
Chapter 8	107
Chapter 9	113
Chapter 10	121

Chapter 11	127
Chapter 12	135
Chapter 13	143
Chapter 14	153
Appendix: Amyraut at Alençon	163
Bibliography	171
Index of Scripture	181
Index of Names	185

Illustrations

Amyraut's *Brief Treatise* (French title page)	37
Amyraut's *Defence of Calvin* (French title page)	38
Amyraut's 'place' beside Calvin in Geneva (Museum of the Reformation)	39
Amyraut's *Brief Traitte* on his chair (Museum of the Reformation)	39
Amyraut walked here (Saumur Academy entrance)	40

Acknowledgements

For the type-setting, layout and production of this book the publisher is grateful for the personal interest and professional expertise of Dr Digby James of Quinta Press. Barkers Print & Design are thanked for help with formatting the cover and the facilities provided by Lightning Source are much appreciated.

INTRODUCTION

The work which you hold in your hand is priceless. It is priceless not because it is intrinsically more valuable than any other great work of the seventeenth century or beyond, or because it is a free book to you the interested reader–you have paid an exact, fair price in acquiring this copy no doubt—but this text is priceless rather because not everybody gets a second chance to be heard in this lifetime. For most of us, God grants a short season in this life in which we find our usefulness for His kingdom and then, well, we expire; sadly, most of us will be unreservedly forgotten after we leave this earth. Our ideas, our works, our impact in our generation, and our voices are extinguished for the ages when we die. Forgotten, we are relegated to the annals of history, and then most of the world will never know we even existed. However, this is not always true! For some, for those that God would use to be a voice of change and hope for many generations after them, their voices, though faint, are still heard. This is the case with Moses Amyraut (French spelling is Moïse Amyraut), a seventeenth century (1596–1664) Frenchman whose voice carries on today with a message as relevant as the day he penned these words.

This work in your hands, *A Brief Treatise*, therefore, represents a priceless reality. For the first time in some three hundred and eighty years, a brilliant theologian, pastor, political and spiritual leader of the French Reformed Church gets to be heard again in his own voice, a fresh voice to a new generation with ideas that have perplexed those within the Protestant Reformed tradition and those outside of Protestantism. Moses Amyraut's voice was desperately needed as a moderating influence in his own polemical context in seventeenth century France where he was helping develop theology within the Reformed Tradition and among those French Roman Catholic leaders and masses who were so profoundly confused about the nature and doctrine of predestination. This preliminary work of Amyraut attempts to teach, encourage, and inspire the reader, be they Protestant or Roman

Catholic, Reformed or Arminian, Christian or Seeker, to think critically with him about God's very gracious nature in the work of redemption known briefly as the doctrine of predestination, fixed within the taxonomy of soteriology or the study of salvation.

This work by Amyraut was needed for his generation. And with a fresh and critical translation into modern English, Amyraut's voice is needed for this current generation who are asking themselves the very same questions and struggling through the same arguments concerning the nature of God, the doctrine of predestination, and the extent of Christ's atonement. Some may even argue that today's theological discussions concerning biblical predestination and the nature of Christ's atonement are even more dynamic and relevant than in Amyraut's day since so much is at stake globally with the need for world evangelization, biblical teaching in a post-Christian world, and global ministry to the masses with a Christo-centric, God-exalting, biblically based theology. Yet, regarding these eternal subjects, Amyraut has had much to say and add to the ongoing theological conversation for nearly four hundred years. Amyraut still has much to say. Thus, it is time to hear Amyraut's passion and voice on these life-giving matters.

Unfortunately, during the last four centuries, the great majority of critics of Amyraut have ignored, excoriated, and dismissed his theological ideas as either irrelevant or heretical depending on the theological tradition in which these critics found themselves. Yet, deeply more concerning than the rejection of Amyraut's temperate theological stance within the Reformed Tradition (being the very Father of Moderate Calvinism), and because this first of Amyraut's polemical works was not readily accessible over the centuries and since also this original (1634) edition of the *Brief Treatise on Predestination* was written in Middle French, very few have *ever even read Amyraut* as a primary source! And having never read Amyraut themselves, these critics, depending on secondary and tertiary biased sources, have somehow felt justified in completely rejecting his theological arguments and doctrinal position outright, as truly uncritical and irresponsible as that sounds for any honest intellectual to undertake. Thus, in hope of righting this wrong for the current and following generations of interested readers, new theologians and pastors, informed laity and critics alike, Amyraut's voice in this work *A Brief Treatise* is now available to be heard again and his ideas and passion are able to be read anew for the generations to come.

In his own generation, Moses Amyraut's work was a labor of love for His

Savior toward the many who were confused concerning how God works in the saving of the soul and of God's desire to do so for His own glory. Today, this new translation of Amyraut into modern English is as needed and useful for today's generation of scholars, pastors, and laymen as it was when it was first penned in 1634 as a quick, "*Brief,*" overview of the foundational nature of God's saving work as described in the word "predestination;" predestination is a word which comports that in God's perfect and mysterious sovereignty He sent His Son Jesus to die on the cross and proffered Christ's death as a perfect, universal atonement for mankind's sin while drawing and applying that precious atonement to God's elect through the regenerative work of the Holy Spirit. Since this Trinitarian truth is so confounding, accurately described as both a veritable mystery and a profound mercy never to be fully grasped in one's lifetime—along with the gross misrepresentations in Amyraut's day of a predestination which only showed God as a harsh, exacting despot—Amyraut wrote this treatise to calm fears, to assuage confusion, to show God's biblical nature in a clearer, softer manner as a merciful God who desires to save all—while equally enunciating the biblical reality that man must truly appreciate his own grave situation, a depraved nature, and his responsibility to accept Christ as Savior if he would be eternally saved. In short, this *Brief Treatise* is both theological and evangelistic in its purpose, as Amyraut desired to help others better understand the loving God of Scripture and engender a right view of God's nature for both Roman Catholics and those within the Protestant Reformed tradition, all while passionately inviting the world to believe and trust in Jesus as their Savior so as to be wonderfully saved. As history affirms, Amyraut's work was used greatly by God in his generation to do exactly that.

May God continue to use this little treatise to light a fire of hope in your life to examine the realities of God's nature, of God's overt mercy in the saving of not only humanity in general through the atoning work of Jesus on the cross, but in God's desire to rescue and redeem for all eternity even you, the reader. May God use Amyraut's words to show you a clear picture of the gospel, of the hope only found in Jesus Christ. May the Lord bless all who undertake to read, absorb, and propagate Amyraut's voice as a means of sharing God's love and mercy with the world and educating sons and daughters in the truth of God's Word that many would find Christ as Savior! So, let Amyraut speak; let his voice be heard again that through Christ and God's eternal truth found in the doctrine of predestination many may be entirely converted to Jesus as Savior and God forever glorified. Sola Gloria Deo.

A QUICK LOOK AT AMYRAUT[1]

There are many who would dismiss our conference as an unwelcome and undesirable event in the Reformed Evangelical calendar. Generally dismissing Amyraldianism as a compromise between Arminianism and Calvinism, they fear a dilution and weakening of what they regard as 'orthodox' Calvinism. However, I believe that sufficient has been written within the last four decades at least to demonstrate that Amyraldian theology is both a reaffirmation of Calvin's original teaching[2] and, more importantly, a confirmation of the true message of the Word of God.[3] Yet, Amyraut continues to have a bad press. In systematic theologies and articles, his distinctive theological stance is usually misrepresented and marginalised.[4] As if the man had openly spurned the Reformation doctrine of Justification by Faith,[5] he is—in some circles at least—having difficulty in shaking off the unflattering epithet of 'the grave digger of the French Reformed Church',[6] a charge repeated as recently as 2003.[7]

For the vast majority of students of church history and Christian biography, the Huguenot Amyraut (1596–1664) is an unknown figure compared with

---

1   A paper given at the 4th Amyraldian Association Conference held at Attleborough, Norfolk on 5 April 2006.

2   See especially Brian G. Armstrong, *Calvinism and the Amyraut Heresy: Protestant Scholasticism and Humanism in Seventeenth-Century France* (Madison: University of Wisconsin Press, 1969); see also further bibliographical data and argument in my *Calvinus* (Norwich: Charenton Reformed Publishing, 1996) and *Amyraut Affirmed* (Norwich: Charenton Reformed Publishing, 2004).

3   For a recent summary, see Paul T. Nimmo & David A. S. Ferguson, *Reformed Theology* (Cambridge: CUP, 2016), 52–3.

4   See L. Berkhof, *Systematic Theology* (London: The Banner of Truth Trust, 1958), 394 and R. L. Reymond, *New Systematic Theology of the Christian Faith* (Nashville: Thomas Nelson, 1998), 475–9. I have responded to these 'standard' dismissals in several publications (see note 2).

5   See Amyraut's concurrence with Calvin on this subject in Armstrong, 222ff.

6   See my refutation of this absurd accusation in *Calvinus*, 16 and *Amyraut Affirmed*, 52.

7   See Ian Hamilton, *Amyraldianism—is it modified Calvinism?* (Worcester: Evangelical Presbyterian Church in England and Wales, 2003), 26.

someone like his near-contemporary, the Puritan Richard Baxter (1615–91). Yet within a British historical context, Richard Baxter is generally regarded as the chief exponent of Amyraldianism. Even though, at one time, Baxter's doctrinal distinctives were identified as 'Baxterianism',[1] he tends to be styled as an 'Amyraldian'. Who then is the Frenchman whose teaching gave our English Baxter his theological identity? As we all should know, the Puritan is far from being a shadowy figure. His extraordinary ministry in seventeenth-century Kidderminster is celebrated by an appropriate local statue; his nationwide influence was diffused by such still-gripping page turners as *The Saints' Everlasting Rest* and *Call to the Unconverted;* and his lovely hymn 'Ye holy angels bright' is still enjoyed by modern worshippers. Neither must we ignore that his colourful and dramatic life is recorded in his autobiography with its exotic Latin title *Reliquiae Baxterianae*. Lastly, Baxter made a further mark on English church history by his courageous stand before the infamous Judge Jeffreys in 1685.

Turning to Moïse Amyraut, while he had an effective pastoral ministry, he never quite turned Saumur upside down, and this charming town in the Loire Valley exhibits no statue to commemorate him. Although he wrote a series of highly-significant theological works, he wrote no devotional or evangelistic classic, neither is a little-known hymn ever sung. Lastly, no *Reliquiae Amyraldianae* exists to perpetuate his memory. Our ignorance is chiefly due more to prejudice than the language and culture barrier, more formidable perhaps to overcome than the geological problems faced by the builders of the Channel Tunnel. On top of the 'foreign' nature of some features of French culture is French religion in general and that of Huguenot history in particular. This is where an almost unknown Englishman comes to our aid. I refer to a certain John Quick, the mere mention of whose name should explain the wording of my title. In short, my paper is not a ten-minute *hors d'oeuvre*!

My known passionate affinities with the Huguenots are due neither to Francophilia as such nor to French Protestant ancestry. For all that my roots are English, my interests are self-consciously spiritual and theological. If any precedents are needed for my enthusiasm, I would cite such English

---

1 See G. F. Nuttall, *Richard Baxter and Philip Doddridge: a Study in a Tradition* (London: Dr Williams's Library, 1954).

nineteenth-century writers as Samuel Smiles[1] and Richard Heath[2] if not the American historian Henry Baird (probably of Scottish descent). All these authors wrote significant accounts of the Huguenots, especially the latter whose comprehensive six-volume history was published between 1880 and 1895.[3] However, I feel a close affinity with the aforementioned English Presbyterian minister John Quick (1636–1706), the tercentenary of whose death falls later this month. This persecuted puritan was the first writer to chronicle and document the Huguenot epic for English readers in an extensive manner.[4] Being both a personally-acquainted commentator on their affairs and a participant in the struggles of English Nonconformity, Quick is a literary 'link man' and part of the broader story at the same time. So, before we take a look at Quick's look at Amyraut, it is necessary to take a 'quick look at Quick'![5]

The reason for John Quick's inclusion in our story will be apparent from a sketch of his little-known life. He was born at Plymouth in 1636. After graduating at Oxford in 1657 he was ordained at Ermington in Devon in 1659. Along with his illustrious puritan brethren—a more famous contemporary John Flavel (1628–91) ministered at nearby Dartmouth, Quick exercised a faithful and courageous ministry. He served at Kingsbridge with Churchstow and then at Brixton near Plymouth. Undeterred by the Act of Uniformity (1662), he continued to preach. He was arrested during the Lord's Day morning worship on 13 December 1663 and imprisoned at Exeter. At his trial, Quick was nearly acquitted on a technicality. However, since he refused to give up preaching, he was sent to prison. After suffering for a further eight weeks, he was liberated by Sir Matthew Hale. The Bishop of Exeter, Seth Ward then prosecuted Quick for preaching to the prisoners but the Lord's servant was acquitted, his unashamed 'guilt' notwithstanding!

---

1 See *The Huguenots—their settlements, churches, and industries in England and Ireland* (London: John Murray, 1880) and *The Huguenots in France after the Revocation of the Edict of Nantes* (London: Daldy, Isbister & Co., 1875).

2 *The Reformation in France* (London: The Religious Tract Society, 1886), 2 Vols.

3 See *History of the Rise of the Huguenots* (London: Hodder & Stoughton, 1880), 2 Vols; *The Huguenots and Henry of Narvarre* (London: Hodder & Stoughton, 1886), 2 Vols; *The Huguenots and the Revocation of the Edict of Nantes* (London: Hodder & Stoughton, 1895), 2 Vols.

4 In his otherwise excellent study, *Huguenot Heritage: The history and contribution of the Huguenots in Britain* (London: Routledge, 1985), Robin D. Gwyn makes no reference to John Quick.

5 The following material including a portrait may be found in my *Calvin Celebrated: The Genevan Reformer & His Huguenot Sons* (Norwich: Charenton Reformed Publishing, 2009), 52ff.

King Charles II's indulgence of 1672 brought a brief respite for the persecuted puritan brotherhood. Quick was licensed to preach at Plymouth. When restrictions were imposed again the following year, he was imprisoned for three months with other nonconformists at the Marshalsea prison in Plymouth. On his release, Quick left the west of England for London. He then travelled to the Netherlands where he became a minister to the English church at Middleburg in 1679. Returning to London two years later, Quick gathered a Presbyterian congregation in a small meeting house in Middlesex Court, Bartholomew Close, Smithfield. On the eve of less troubled times, his London ministry—'successful to the conversion of many', said Dr Edmund Calamy—was relatively undisturbed. The 'Glorious Revolution' (1688) and the Toleration Act (1689) eventually brought persecution to an end. Known as a 'serious, good preacher' with a 'great facility and freedom in prayer', John Quick continued to serve his people faithfully until his death on 29 April 1706. He was buried in the Dissenters' burial ground at Bunhill Fields. His wife Elizabeth died in 1708. Their only daughter became the wife of Dr John Evans (1680?–1730) who completed the commentary on the Epistle to the Romans in Matthew Henry's immortal *Exposition*.

During his early ministry and subsequently, Quick became acquainted with the Huguenot refugees, some of whom landed at his native Plymouth from La Rochelle in 1681—the year the dreadful 'dragonnades' began. Accordingly, wrote Calamy, Quick 'was very compassionate to those in distress; at a great deal of pains and expense for the relief of the poor French Protestants, and his house and purse were almost ever open to them. He was a perfect master of their language, and had a peculiar respect for their churches, upon the account of their sound doctrine and useful discipline, and the noble testimony which they bore to religion by their sufferings'.

Consistent with his personal courage and pastoral gifts, John Quick combined scholarship with zeal for the truth. The blending of these qualities explains his authorship of a work of major Huguenot interest, the *Synodicon in Gallia Reformata*. This pair of fascinating folios was published in 1692. The work chiefly consists of the proceedings of all the National synods—twenty-nine in all—of the French Reformed Churches from the first held at Paris in 1559 to the last permitted by Louis XIV at Loudun in 1659. Besides an historical introduction, Quick included the Confession of Faith and Discipline of the Reformed Churches together with the Edict of Nantes (1598) and the Edict of Fontainebleau (1685) commonly known as the 'Revocation of the Edict of Nantes'. Pope Innocent XI's congratulatory letter to the French king is also included along with an account of the dreadful persecution of the immediate post-revocation period. The author's title-page claim—'A work never before extant in any language'—is noteworthy. A French 'edition' was later published at the Hague in 1710 by Jean Aymon. Unlike Aymon, Quick had direct access to original manuscript material borrowed from Huguenot refugees which he then collated and translated. Aymon then re-translated Quick's work back into French—which explains his repetition of some of Quick's inaccuracies! The *Synodicon* remains therefore a primary English source for Huguenot information during the early modern period.

Quick's interest in the Huguenots did not end with the *Synodicon*. Besides a few published sermons of his own, he also prepared for publication a selection of fifty brief—some quite lengthy—biographies of eminent pastors, theologians and martyrs of the French Reformed churches, the *Icones Sacrae Gallicanae*. He also produced a similar selection of twenty Puritans, the *Icones Sacrae Anglicanae*. These ambitious ventures failed with the death in 1700 of William Russell, Duke of Bedford (the dedicatee of the *Synodicon*) who had offered to finance the project. Advancing illness also prevented Quick from collecting subscriptions for the work. Following the author's death, the manuscript volumes were eventually deposited at what is now known as Dr Williams's Library. There they remain in their unpublished state although, since the originals decayed with time, a transcription was made of them in the nineteenth century by the Revd Hugh Hutton, MA, minister of Churchgate Presbyterian Church, Bury St Edmunds. The work took three years (1862–5), for which the then princely sum of £150 was paid!

This brings us to the thirty-fifth of Quick's fifty Huguenot biographies or *Icones*: 'The Life of Mons[r]. Amyraut, Pastor and professor in the Church and University of Saumur'. Interestingly, in the two major studies of Amyraut during the last fifty years by Dr Brian G. Armstrong[1] and Dr Frans Pieter van Stam,[2] this work was neglected. While Quick's *Synodicon* is frequently cited, his *Icones Sacrae Gallicanae* are ignored.[3] However, biographical information is

---

1 See Armstrong, *Calvinism and the Amyraut Heresy: Protestant Scholasticism and Humanism in Seventeenth-Century France* (Madison: University of Wisconsin Press, 1969).

2 *The Controversy over the Theology of Saumur, 1635–1650: Disrupting Debates among the Huguenots in Complicated Circumstances* (Amsterdam & Maarsen: APA–Holland University Press, 1988).

3 Armstrong was aware of the work (see 292) but he neither quotes it nor cites it in his bibliography (at 300). For Quick's *Icone* of Amyraut at Dr Williams's Library, see DWL 6, 38–39 (35).

cited from Pierre Bayle's *Dictionnaire historique et critique* (1696),[1] described by Armstrong as 'an under-valued and under-used source containing much that is still important and not readily accessible elsewhere'.[2] For information about Amyraut, Bayle states that his source was 'the memoirs communicated by M. Amyraut the son', a source also used by Quick. However, the latter's biography includes more personal features than Bayle revealed in his *Dictionnaire*. These generally unknown 'personal features' are a vital part of this presentation of Amyraut's life.

His ancestors coming originally from Alsace and later Orleans, Moïse Amyraut was born in September 1596 at Bourgueil in Anjou, a small town in the Loire Valley 40 km west of Tour. Provided an education in the humanities, his father sent him to study law at the university of Poitiers. Proving himself a diligent student working daily for 14 hours, Moïse graduated Licentiate after a year. Travelling home via Saumur, he visited M. Bouchereau, pastor of the Reformed Church, who recognised the young man's extraordinary abilities and piety. Being introduced to the Governor of Saumur, the famous Huguenot soldier-statesman and scholar The Lord Philippe du Plessis-Mornay, young Moïse was encouraged to abandon law and study theology. At first reluctant, his father agreed with the advice given. Studying other works by Tully, Demosthenes and Aristotle, Moïse felt drawn to theology and the Christian ministry through reading John Calvin's *Institutes of the Christian Religion*. He was admitted to the Reformed Academy at Saumur, founded by Lord du Plessis-Mornay in 1599. Moïse thus came under the influence of the Scottish theologian John Cameron (c. 1580–1625) who served as Professor of Theology from 1618–21. Cameron had a profound influence on Moïse who became his most famous pupil. Succeeding the Dutch Francis Gomarus at Saumur, Cameron challenged the ultra-orthodox theology of Calvin's successor Theodore Beza. Restless and outspoken, he became known as 'Bezae mastyx' or 'Beza's scourge'. Effectively signalling a return to the balanced biblicism of Calvin, Amyraut embraced and developed Cameron's 'authentic Calvinism', a *via media* between Arminianism and Bezaism. Such

---

1 See English translation: *The Dictionary Historical and Critical of Mr Peter Bayle* (London: 1734). References to the article on Amyraut in Volume 1 hereafter cited as 'Bayle'.

2 *Calvinism and the Amyraut Heresy*, 300. For Bayle, see Elizabeth Labrousse, *Bayle* (Oxford: OUP, 1983).

was Amyraut's admiration for Cameron that he imitated his gestures and even spoke French with a Scottish accent![1]

Little information is available about Amyraut for the years 1618–26. However, in 1626, he was called to succeed his life-long friend and former fellow student Jean Daillé as pastor at Saumur. Having commenced his ministry in the town in 1625, Daillé—the future preacher *par excellence*—was called to the great Reformed Temple at Charenton near Paris where he exercised a powerful and influential ministry until his death in 1670.[2] Having authored his first major publication *A Treatise Concerning Religions* (1631),[3] Amyraut was appointed as theology professor in the Academy in 1631. He joined the learned Hebraist Louis Capell and fellow theologian Josué de la Place[4] on the faculty. All three being disciples of Cameron, they exhibited a remarkable harmony 'as is rarely to be met with in academic land' says Bayle.[5] Writing more quaintly, Quick states that 'it was commonly said of them, that their three heads were covered with one bonnet, i. e. with one and the same nightcap'.[6]

Before we proceed, it is important to remember the religious and political context in which the Huguenots lived.[7] While they were a sizeable and significant minority, their liberties within Roman Catholic France were defined by the Edict of Nantes, granted during the reign of Henri IV in 1598.

1　Bayle, ii. 288–9.

2　For Daillé, see Bayle, ii. 580ff; Quick, *Icones*, 39; also my *Calvin Celebrated: The Genevan Reformer & His Huguenot Sons* (Norwich: Charenton Reformed Publishing, 2009), 8off.

3　Traitté des religions contre ceux qui les estiment toutes indifferentes (Saumur: Girard & de Lerpiniere, 1631); English translation full title: A Treatise Concerning Religions, in Refutation of the Opinion which accounts all indifferent, wherein is also evinced the necessity of a Particular Revelation, And the Verity and preeminence of the Christian Religion above the Pagan, Mahometan, and Jewish rationally Demonstrated (London: 1660). See also David Llewellyn Jenkins, 'Amyraut on other Religions' in Christ for the World, Amyraldian Association Conference Report (Norwich: Charenton Reformed Publishing, 2007), 44–91.

4　See David Llewellyn Jenkins, *Saumur Redux: Josué de la Place & the Question of Adam's Sin* (Harleston, Norfolk: Leaping Cat Press, 2008).

5　Bayle, 261.

6　*Icones*, 962.

7　For a modern study, see Geoffrey Treasure, *The Huguenots* (New Haven and London: Yale University Press, 2013); also Mack P. Holt, ed., *Renaissance and Reformation in France* (Oxford: OUP, 2002); see also H. O. Wakeman, *The Ascendancy of France, 1598–1715* (London: Rivingtons, 1959); for an earlier useful overview, see A. J. Grant, *The Huguenots* (London: Thornton Butterworth/ Oxford: OUP, 1934).

After decades of religious conflict, the Edict guaranteed a degree of religious freedom and other public privileges. However, due to constant intrigue by the Jesuits and other Roman Catholic conservatives, the position of the Huguenots still made them vulnerable. As 'second class citizens', they enjoyed a fragile and frequently-violated peace. To practise the Reformed religion always demanded a combination of courage and wisdom. Throughout their public lives and ministries, the Huguenot pastors generally proved exemplary in this respect. It was during the National Synod of Charenton (1631) that Amyraut made his initial mark. Contrary to earlier custom, the Reformed delegates from the previous National Synod of Castres (1626) presented their complaints and grievances over violations of the Edict of Nantes before King Louis XIII *on their knees*. Determined to honour the King yet maintain their privileges as servants of Christ, Amyraut insisted that he would address His Majesty *standing*. Thus commissioned by the Synod, so he did. In fact, so impressive was Amyraut's demeanour in the whole matter, his courage, manners and integrity won him the esteem of Cardinal Richelieu.

Amyraut is chiefly remembered for setting the cat among the pigeons over the theology of predestination. When a Roman Catholic nobleman—otherwise sympathetic to the Reformed Faith—expressed doubts about what he perceived to be Calvin's teaching, Amyraut responded with his first work on the subject. However, his *Brief Treatise on Predestination* (1634)[1] aroused the wrath of the Reformed world when he expounded a position on election, the extent of the atonement and 'universal grace' at odds with accepted wisdom. Starting what Bayle described as a 'kind of civil war among the Protestant divines of France',[2] it soon became clear that Amyraut—heavily influenced by Calvin—was pursuing a very different theological agenda from 'orthodox' theologians like the 'French John Owen' Pierre du Moulin, but one that was not exposed to many of the *biblical* objections raised by many then and subsequently.

Rooted in a dualistic conception of the divine will (see *Deuteronomy 29:29*), Calvin taught that Christ was offered as the Redeemer of the whole world according to God's 'revealed' conditional will albeit only received by elected believers according to God's 'hidden' absolute will. Notwithstanding the rationally-challenging paradox involved, Calvin maintained the doctrines of

---

[1] *Brief Traitté de la predestination et de ses principales dependences* (Saumur: Isaac Desbordes, 1634).
[2] Bayle, 261.

universal atonement and divine election side by side. Faced by clear biblical evidence for both, he refused to tamper with the scriptural texts. Logic was not allowed to dictate one emphasis at the expense of the other. Typical of his numerous statements on the extent of the atonement, Calvin commented thus on Romans 5:18: 'Paul makes grace common to all, not because it in fact extends to all, but because it is offered to all. Although Christ suffered for the sins of the world, and is offered by the goodness of God without distinction to all men, yet not all receive him'.[1]

Unhappy with this kind of dualism, Calvin's rationalistic successor Theodore Beza deleted the 'universal' aspect of Calvin's scheme in favour of limited atonement, which in turn provoked the equally-rationalistic Jakob Arminius to delete the 'particular' aspect of Calvin's scheme in favour of conditional election. Unimpressed by either of the two deviants, Amyraut was persuaded that Calvin's original position alone possessed biblical integrity. For him, the only option was Calvin's 'authentic Calvinism'. Amyraut also insisted that Calvin's view, with its unique 'mind and heart-set', had enormous pastoral and evangelistic advantages. Roger Nicole admits that Calvin's comment on Romans 5:18 'comes perhaps closest to providing support for Amyraut's thesis'.[2] Even Richard Muller admits that 'Calvin's teaching was ... capable of being cited with significant effect by Moïse Amyraut against his Reformed opponents'.[3] According to Dr van Stam, at a time when Bezan ultra-orthodoxy had replaced Calvin's balanced biblicism, 'Amyraut ... revealed the attraction which the theology of Calvin held for him. He demonstrated this preference in an array of books, in the process proving his familiarity with the writings of this reformer. ... Amyraut rediscovered Calvin, as it were, and was perhaps the Calvin-expert of the day. In any case, Amyraut fell under the spell of Calvin's theology'.[4] Thus historian Philip Benedict—who incorrectly imagines the Canons of the Synod of Dort (1618–19) to represent a *higher* orthodoxy than is the case—recognises

---

1   *Comment* on Romans 5:18.

2   Dr Nicole flies in the face of the obvious when he adds: 'it may well refer simply to the relevance of the sacrifice of Christ to a universal offer, without actually asserting a substitutionary suffering for all mankind' (*Moyse Amyraut (1596–1664) and the Controversy on Universal Grace* (Harvard University thesis, 1966), 83, n. 38).

3   *The Unaccommodated Calvin* (Oxford: OUP, 2000), 62.

4   *The Controversy over the Theology of Saumur* (Amsterdam & Maarssen: APA–Holland University Press 1988), 431.

Amyraut's position in France accurately when he says that 'the theologians of the Academy of Saumur ... consciously opposed Beza and appealed to Calvin instead. ... In effect they reversed the steps that had been taken in the passage from Calvin to Calvinism'.[1]

Amyraut's impeccable *authentic* Calvinist orthodoxy did not shield him from the charge of Arminianising heresy, even though he claimed an orthodoxy consistent with the Canons of Dort. He—with his fellow pastor Paul Testard of Blois who had also published a similarly 'heretical' piece—was tried and acquitted at the National Synod of Alençon (1637). The controversy was to rumble on for decades, not only in France but throughout Europe and beyond. Even today, ultra-orthodox blood pressure is often raised when anyone dares to defend and expound the tenets of Moïse Amyraut. Sadly, for most students of French church history, knowledge of Amyraut is confined to his theological notoriety. Since these theological issues are discussed in depth elsewhere, we will continue to explore the less-familiar features of Amyraut's life.

Returning home from the Synod of Alençon, all Saumur rejoiced at Amyraut's acquittal. The Academy flourished for many years with many students attending from all parts of France and beyond. Indeed, the Saumur Academy became the premier institution of its kind. Amyraut's personal reputation grew with the years, not least among the Roman Catholics. As we have noted, the King's chief minister Cardinal Richelieu greatly admired him.

What is striking is the way Amyraut maintained his Reformed convictions without compromise. Surrounded as the Reformed community in France was by a large and not always benign Roman Catholic majority, tensions were not always easy to handle, even during the 'golden years' (1629–61).[2] However, in the true spirit of the Gospel, Amyraut avoided the extremes of social hostility and a servile ecumenism. He demonstrated this when, to ingratiate himself at Rome, the Cardinal advanced a scheme to unite the Roman and Reformed communions in France. He commissioned the Jesuit Father Audebert to sound out the Reformed pastors. Intending to engage in talks with Amyraut, the Jesuit visited Saumur. Brought together by the King's Lieutenant, M. Villeneuve, Father Audebert soon discovered that Amyraut

---

1 *The Faith and Fortunes of France's Huguenots, 1600–85* (Aldershot: Ashgate, 2001), 227.

2 See Menna Prestwich, 'The Huguenots under Richelieu and Mazarin, 1629–61: A Golden Age?' in Irene Scouloudi, ed., *Huguenots in Britain and their French Background, 1550–1800* (London: Macmillan Press, 1987).

was quite inflexible. Regarding unity, the latter declared 'That this was a thing more to be wished than hoped for; that the opinions of both were so opposite that there was no probability nor possibility of concerting and adjusting them'.[1] When the Jesuit indicated that the Roman Catholics were ready to abandon the invocation of saints, the merit of good works, purgatory and papal supremacy, Amyraut was not to be taken in. These concessions were too few if they did not include the doctrine of the real presence in the Mass. At this point the Romanist refused to yield. Amyraut concluded the discussion insisting that without this, any unity was 'mere vanity'.[2]

Doctrinal debate over the doctrines of grace involved Amyraut in further controversy in the 1640s. When the English Arminian Samuel Hoard, Rector of Morton in Essex published an attack on predestination,[3] the impact of the work was also felt in France. Just as the English 'proto-Amyraldian' John Davenant replied to Hoard, so did Amyraut. It is fascinating to discover that both authors did not refute Hoard from a *Bezan* perspective.[4] They were conscious of doing so as 'authentic Calvinists'.[5] Amyraut could not have been more explicit in calling his reply *A Defence of the Doctrine of Calvin*.[6] Armstrong states that in this work, 'Amyraut clearly identifies his own teaching with that of Calvin. Of all his writings, this is the most important in demonstrating the distinctives of Amyraldianism as compared to the scholastic orientation of the orthodox'.[7] Persisting in the same stance that produced the heresy trial at Alençon in 1637, it was inevitable that Amyraut's critics would try to make more trouble for him at the next National Synod at Charenton in

---

1 *Icones*, 970.

2 Ibid. 970–1.

3 *God's Love to Mankind, manifested by disproving his absolute Decree for their Damnation* (London: 1633).

4 See my introduction to the Quinta Press edition of John Davenant's, *A Dissertation on the Death of Christ* (Weston Rhyn: Quinta Press, 2006).

5 See *Animadversions written by the Right Rev. Father in God, John, Lord Bishop of Salisbury, upon a treatise intituled, God's Love to Mankind* (Cambridge: 1641), 142.

6 Published first in Latin as *Defensio doctrinae J. Calvini de absoluto reprobationis decreto* (Saumur, 1641), the work appeared three years later in French as *Defense de la doctrine de Calvin* (Saumur: Isaac Desbordes, 1644).

7 *Calvinism and the Amyraut Heresy*, 99–100. For an Amyraut bibliography, see Armstrong, 290–8. Archbishop Marsh's Library in Dublin 'contains the largest single collection of the writings of Moyse Amyraut' (*Marsh's Library 1701–2001 Exhibition Catalogue* (Dublin: 2001), 154).

1644–5. As before, all attempts to discredit him proved fruitless.[1] Doubtless influenced by Amyraut's criticisms of Islam in his first major work,[2] this synod drew up a liturgy for receiving converted Muslims into membership of the Reformed Churches.[3]

This synod provides us with a glimpse of Amyraut's magnanimous nature when he defended his Saumur colleague Josué de la Place's views over the doctrine of imputed guilt. Properly speaking, Amyraut defended his friend's right to hold such a view (which again can claim some degree of precedent in Calvin!) even though he did not share it. He simply did not consider it sufficiently fundamental to dispute about publicly, and his eloquence won the day.

More important to his ongoing ministry among the churches, Amyraut was asked to write a 'paraphrase or commentary' on the Bible. He commenced this in 1644 with his commentary on Romans. Eventually he covered all the epistles, the Acts of the Apostles and the Gospel of John. He died before attempting a harmony of the Gospels. Like Calvin, he declined to do anything on the Book of Revelation.[4]

Personal tragedy hit the Amyrauts in 1645 when their only daughter died at the age of nineteen. To comfort his distressed wife, Amyraut wrote his *Treatise on the State of Believers after Death*.[5] Not initially intended for publication, it was only printed when others, impressed by the therapeutic quality of the work, urged him to do so. Published in 1646, it was translated into English and German. In this work, Amyraut the theologian was also Amyraut the pastor. Combining faithful exegesis with deep sympathy, he was able to minister effectively to the bereaved.

Amyraut was remarkable for the way he combined academic concerns and pastoral compassion. Many besides his students sought his wise solutions to their intellectual and personal perplexities. The Roman Catholics of Saumur knew that when students of their college had disputes with those of the Reformed Academy, they could rely on Amyraut to be reliable umpire.

---

1 See Quick, *Synodicon*, ii. 455.
2 See Amyraut, *Traitté des religions contre ceux qui les estiment toutes indifferentes* (Saumur: Girard & de Lerpiniere, 1631).
3 See Quick, *Synodicon*, ii. 449.
4 Quick, *Icones*, 976.
5 *Discours de l'estat des fideles apres la mort* (Saumur: Jean Lesnier, 1646); tr: *The Evidence of things not seen, or Diverse ... Discourses Concerning the State of Good and Holy Men after Death* (London, n. d.).

He was famous for his philanthropy to the poor, irrespective of religious affiliation. When the local monastery was burned down, the friars asked him to approach M. Hervart, the King's Controller of Revenue—who happened to be a Reformed man—to help with rebuilding costs. Quick tells us that 'the begging friars would be sure to knock at his doors, for they never missed of a good alms, their knapsacks being well filled. And he would tell them pleasantly, that he gave them candles that they might read more and study better'.[6]

Quick provides a challenging and beautiful picture of Amyraut the model pastor:

> The poor of both religions loved and reverenced him as their common father, for he distributed his charity indifferently among them all. But yet he had a most particular concern for the sick, and how many and urgent so ever his businesses were, they should never dispense with him from visiting them on their beds of languishing, and administering spiritual physic, counsels and comforts suitable to their conditions and inward circumstances. He evaded not this office and service of love, neither for the sultry heats of the day, nor for the storms and bitter colds of the night. He hath quitted his own bed and repose to console dying persons'.[7]

As we discover the gracious character of Moïse Amyraut, it is important to repeat that he always maintained his Reformed convictions without compromise. For him, a compassionate heart and a sound head were not—as is often the case today—mutually exclusive. He proved this in June 1646 when, by order of the Privy Council, during the Roman Catholic Festival of Corpus Christi,[8] the Reformed families of Saumur were ordered to hang tapestries from their balconies as the idolatrous procession passed along the streets of the town. For Amyraut, this situation was a test case for Reformed fidelity. Responding to the instruction of the Seneschal—the chief judge of the city—that Amyraut should direct the Protestant people to obey the order, we see evidence of old-fashioned Calvinist courage. Quick's account reveals something of the drama and tension involved:

---

6 *Icones*, 977.
7 Ibid. 978.
8 Falling on the first Thursday after Trinity Sunday, the festival involved a colourful and pompous procession led by priests carrying what Quick calls 'their breaden God' consecrated in the Mass.

[Amyraut] had indeed always preached up subjection unto the higher powers, but then it was in those matters in which conscience was not interested nor concerned, that he was so far from exhorting his flock to yield obedience in this case, that he would go immediately unto every house of the Reformed, and particularly charge them not in the least to obey this wicked order, nor in any wise to yield the least consent unto it, whatever they might suffer for it. And that he would be the first to give them an example and pattern of steadfastness and constancy, and patience in their religion. What he said he did. M. Amyraut was as good as his word. For he was not a reed shaken with the wind; but fixed and immovable in his holy purpose and resolutions as a rock. He therefore quits the High Priest's Hall, the Seneschal's house, and goes from house to house, admonishing and warning all his flock not to have to do in any wise with this idolatry. God's glory and the everlasting salvation of their precious souls were now at stake. They should quit themselves as men, as the ancient saints of God had done before them, rather suffer than sin, burn in the furnace than bow the knee to the King's golden image or impious decree.[1]

Such was the example of one decried as 'the grave digger of the French Reformed Church'!

The Corpus Christi episode illustrates the dilemma constantly facing the Huguenots. In their obedience to the Word of God, they always sought to 'Fear God' and 'Honour the King' (*1 Peter 2:17*). In matters not involving religious conformity they endeavoured to be model subjects. Thus far they were happy to be 'politically correct'. However, should the King command anything contrary to their consciences as Reformed Christians, Peter's bold stand was theirs also: 'We ought to obey God rather than men' (*Acts 5:29*). As Amyraut's behaviour made clear, the Huguenot was guided by 'Christian correctness', a stance which in no way could properly be construed as 'revolutionary'. Such was the influential teaching expounded in the final chapter of John Calvin's *Institutes*. While leaving room for the legitimacy of 'popular magistrates' in their *public capacity* to 'curb the tyranny of kings',[2] the duty of *private* Christians is to 'prove our obedience to them, whether

---

1 *Icones*, 978–80.
2 *Institutes*, IV. xx. 31.

in complying with edicts, or in paying tribute'[1] and cooperating in other civil matters.

Faced by royal tyranny, 'private men' must recognise that while 'the Lord takes vengeance on unbridled domination', our obligation is to 'obey and suffer'.[2] A faithful exegete of the Word of God, Calvin clearly had a high view of kingship. Citing 1 Peter 2:17 and Proverbs 24:21, he states that 'under the term honour, [the Apostle Peter] includes a sincere and candid esteem, and [Solomon], by joining the king with God, shows that he is invested with a kind of sacred veneration and dignity'.[3] Even when rulers are unjust, 'this feeling of reverence, and even of piety, we owe to the utmost of our rulers, be their characters what they may'.[4] This teaching explains why, after the execution of King Charles I in 1649, Huguenots like Amyraut distanced themselves from the English Puritan regicides. Agreeing with Calvin, Amyraut published his treatise *The Sovereignty of Kings* in 1650.[5] At a time when the political heritage of the United Kingdom is fast becoming an 'anything-goes' 'PC' democratic tyranny, no less hostile to Christians than the monarchical tyrannies of old, the teaching of Calvin and Amyraut is worthy of sober reflection today. Surely, the ultimate issue is not 'monarchy *versus* democracy' but the value consensus shared by both the governors and the governed within society, whatever theory of government operates at any one time.

Because of the religious affinities between the Huguenots and the Puritans (especially the Presbyterians), the English civil war created problems in France. Reformed believers were suspected of fomenting revolution against established order. Unlike England, France had already endured the sixteenth-century wars of religion, and, for Amyraut and his generation, the terrible siege of La Rochelle (1627–8) in which Cardinal Richelieu crushed Protestant political power in France forever, was very recent history. In another work, *An Apology for those of the Reformed Religion*,[6] Amyraut took the view that for all that was noble in Huguenot resistance to royal tyranny, just religious grievances were too often mixed up with dubious politics.

These issues were brought into sharp focus during the civil disturbances

---

1 Ibid. IV. xx. 23.
2 Ibid. IV. xx. 31.
3 Ibid. IV. xx. 22.
4 Ibid. IV. xx. 29.
5 *Discours sur la souveraineté des rois* (Charenton: L. Vendosme, 1650).
6 *Apologie pour ceux de la Religion Reformeé* (Saumur: Isaac Desbordes, 1647).

in France known as the War of the Fronde (1648–53). Succeeding Cardinal Richelieu on his death in 1642 (and Louis XIII died the following year), Cardinal Mazarin's unpopular rule was challenged by the Paris Parlement which sought to limit royal power during the minority of Louis XIV. The revolt being suppressed by the Duke of Condé, he himself led a rebellion in 1650 which ended three years later. The entire conflict was civil rather than religious, being doubtless influenced by events in England. So when Condé used his protestant ancestry to gain Huguenot support in 1651, he was disappointed. Amyraut and his brethren preached obedience to the young King. Their allegiance was considered decisive. Count Harcourt summed up the situation when he declared to the deputies of Montauban, "The crown was tottering on the King's head, but you have steadied it."[1]

Returning from banishment, Cardinal Mazarin was no less grateful to the 'little flock'.[2] In 1652, Louis expressed appreciation for Huguenot support: "Our subjects aforesaid of the Pretended Reformed Religion have afforded us sure proofs of their affection and faithfulness, … wherewith we are much pleased."[3] The King also promised to guarantee the Huguenot privileges provided in the Edict of Nantes. Thus the Huguenots rejoiced. Unlike the English Puritans, they had few misgivings about royalty. At that time, there was no reason to suspect that young Louis would one day become a monster persecutor. However, from 1656 onwards, Louis began to exhibit signs of a change of heart, an intolerant 'absolutist' disposition which eventually led to the terrible Dragonnades of 1681 and Revocation of the Edict of Nantes in 1685.

Amyraut became closely involved with the events of these tumultuous times. In January 1651, the Royal Court came to Saumur. According to custom, there was great pressure on the Reformed community to alter their weekly worship routine during the first three days of the royal visit. Amyraut was prepared to be accommodating on the understanding that their normal Lord's Day services would take place as usual. John Quick provides a fascinating account of what happened next:

> The King came to Saumur the Monday night, and there was no

---

1 Henry M. Baird, *The Huguenots and the Revocation of the Edict of Nantes* (London: Hodder & Stoughton, 1895), i. 395.
2 Ibid.
3 Ibid. 397.

sermon on Wednesday, but on the next Lord's Day the whole service was performed as usual. M. Amyraut preached in the afternoon. The King was just then got into his majority [actually his fourteenth year], and together with several young Lords walked out onto the tennis court, which was near adjoining unto the Temple of the Reformed. The Protestants were then singing the Psalm. The King being a perfect stranger to this action and melody demanded the meaning of it. Somebody answered it was part of the religious worship of the Huguenots. "Let's go in," said the King, "and see what they are doing." But some great ones then about him obstructed his resolution, and conducted him to his sports and divertisements.

One wonders what might have transpired in the soul of young Louis XIV had he come under the ministry of M. Amyraut. Quick continues:

Whilst the King was engaged in his play, some of the courtiers had the curiosity to get into the Temple, and the patience to tarry out the whole sermon. M. Amyraut preached upon those words of St Peter, 'Fear God. Honour the King' [*1 Peter 2:17*]. When the action was ended, they declared their great satisfaction one unto the other, and commended the preacher highly, as a man of singular merit and eloquence. They went directly from the Temple to the racket court, and acquainted His Majesty with that excellent discourse of the Huguenot minister; yea and at night when Her Majesty [the Queen Mother] sat at table she was recreated with the punctual relation of it.[1]

Surprise at Amyraut's preaching is not difficult to explain. Roman Catholic propaganda created the impression that the Huguenots were a perpetual threat to church and state. Confronted by the reality of Huguenot piety, those in a position to judge for themselves were able to draw a different conclusion.

Arriving at Saumur the following week, even Cardinal Mazarin heard about the sermon and wanted to meet the preacher. Meeting at the Cardinal's lodgings, the two men sat by the fire and talked. When Amyraut assured Mazarin of Huguenot support for the King, the Cardinal was surprised and charmed at the manners and wisdom of the Reformed Pastor. A day or two later, while the King was on a hunting trip, the Cardinal visited the nearby Abbey of St Bennet. On returning from his walk, which provided a

---

1 Quick, *Icones*, 987.

panoramic view of Saumur, he asked his host the Count of Comminges where the Reformed Academy was. Pointing it out in the distance, the Cardinal wished to call on Amyraut. Welcomed at the college gate, he was invited to inspect the library. They discussed the Edict of Nantes and the perpetual obligation of the Kings of France to honour it. News of this encounter was the talk of the town. Many were asking what the Cardinal and the Professor discussed. They did not discuss theological differences on this occasion, as Amyraut later made clear. The Count of Guilaut said to the Queen Mother that had they discussed religion, the Cardinal would have more than met his match in M. Amyraut.[1]

Clearly, the Court and the Cardinal were impressed by the piety, learning and integrity of Amyraut. However, while they could not dismiss the Reformed Faith, time was to prove that their hearts remained hostile to the Gospel thus adorned by Amyraut and his brethren.

In the meantime, the Reformed Churches continued to flourish and the pastors enriched one another by periodic fellowship. In 1653, Jean Daillé called at Saumur on his way from Paris to La Rochelle to ordain his son Adrien at the Reformed Temple.[2] Quick reminds us that, since their student days, Amyraut and Daillé had remained 'dear friends'. Regarded as the greatest French preacher since Calvin, Daillé had fully supported his friend in his theological conflicts. Both men owed so much to their benefactor, The Lord du Plessis-Mornay. During this meeting, they enjoyed rich fellowship as guests of the godly noble Lord's grandson Lord de Villarnoul at his chateau at La Forêt-sur-Sèvre in lower Poitou. We may imagine the joys thus shared in the great hall of the chateau. Quick says that 'their discourses and conversation together did ravish and charm that religious family, and all the guests and strangers that had the happiness to be their auditors'.[3]

Quick also supplies a vivid and charming picture of student life at Saumur. He tells us that 'it was a constant custom with M. Amyraut in the summer evenings to walk in the fields about Saumur, especially after supper. He was always attended with some sixty or fourscore students in divinity, who propounded to him all those difficulties and knotty objections which occurred

---

[1] Ibid. 978–92.
[2] See my *Calvin Celebrated: The Genevan Reformer & His Huguenot Sons* (Norwich: Charenton Reformed Publishing, 2009), 82.
[3] *Icones*, 995.

to them in their private studies'.¹ We can imagine the cut and thrust of provocative yet good-humoured discussion as professor and students fired questions at one another. Quick stresses the importance of these nocturnal excursions:

> These exercises did highly improve those young divines in knowledge, judgement, acumen and ability to defend the truth, and refute errors, and many of them afterwards proved most eminent ministers of the Gospel, and victorious champions of our holy Religion against all the subtle Popish aggressors. And it was these evening walks which occasioned the publication of sundry theological dissertations, which he emitted at diverse times from the press into the open world, and which otherwise might have been buried in the graves of perpetual silence.²

In the sharp winter of 1657, Amyraut had a bad fall after leaving the Temple. Carried home in great agony, he was thought to have broken his thigh. All were gravely concerned, including the Roman Catholics, and fear was expressed for his life. As soon as he recovered from shock, 'he began to speak and comfort those that attended him', says Quick, 'telling them that if the Lord should vouchsafe him that favour as to enjoy the benefit of his tongue and understanding to edify his brethren to the last of his life, he should account this the happiest providence which ever had befallen him'.³

Amyraut had actually suffered a hip dislocation and torn ligaments. He was out of action for six months, during which time he attended to his voluminous correspondence, continuing also with his paraphrase on the Acts of the Apostles. Becoming more mobile with the aid of crutches, he was carried from place to place in a Sedan chair. At the end of August, accompanied by his daughter-in-law, he visited the small spa town of Bourbon in Burgundy, famous for its attractive vista of the Loire Valley. During his stay, many Reformed believers gathered in his apartment on the Lord's Day for worship, ministry and fellowship. They were 'edified', says Quick, 'by his excellent and fruitful sermons'.⁴ One sermon in particular was highly

---

1 Ibid.
2 Ibid. The 'sundry theological dissertations' referred to by Quick are the *Theses Salmurienses* published in four volumes (Saumur, 1665; Geneva, 1665).
3 *Icones*, 996.
4 Ibid. 998.

valued. Finding relief from the *eaux de Bourbon*, he drew parallels between the healing effect of the waters and the grace of God in the Gospel.[1]

Making their way to Paris, Amyraut and his daughter-in-law were welcomed by M. Hervart (the King's Controller of Revenue and a Reformed man) at whose residence they stayed for three months. The Princess of Tarente, the godly daughter of the Huguenot Duke de la Force enjoyed their company and especially Amyraut's discussions on theological and devotional matters. Appearing frequently at the great Temple at Charenton, he preached sermons on the glory of Christ and the work of the Holy Spirit, which were published.[2]

Learning from M. Hervart that Amyraut was in town, Cardinal Mazarin welcomed a further opportunity to speak with the Reformed professor. When they first met, the Cardinal's position during the Fronde had been much less secure. Always impressed by Amyraut's personal integrity and learning, and recalling with pleasure his visit to the Saumur Academy and its library, the Cardinal now invited the Huguenot to see his house and library. While relations were respectful and even cordial, it should be remembered that synodical assemblies of the Reformed Churches could only be approved by the Government. During another visit, having been asked by the Reformed consistory of Paris to petition the Cardinal to authorise a new National Synod, Amyraut duly approached him on the subject. Suspicions about Reformed influence always lurking in the background, matters were never plain sailing. However, the Cardinal, urging Amyraut to be patient, invited him to put the request in writing, which he did.

Permission for the National Synod of Loudun was eventually granted. It was to prove the final synod ever allowed by Louis XIV as he increasingly pursued a Jesuit-inspired policy to exterminate the Reformed Churches of France. Indeed, the King and his advisers had good reason to respect Huguenot resolve. When the Synod commenced 'by His Majesty's Permission' on 10 November 1659, the King's Commissioner demanded that the Huguenots should be more submissive to His Majesty and less antagonistic to the Church of Rome. The Synod Moderator, the illustrious M. Jean Daillé rose to the occasion. While he affirmed the loyalty and submission of the Reformed Churches to the King 'as next under God'[3] in all things lawful, he refused to

---

1 *Discours chrestien sur les eaux de Bourbon* (Charenton: A. Cellier, 1658).
2 See *Cinq sermons prononcez a Charenton* (Charenton: A. Cellier, 1658).
3 *Synodicon*, ii. 511.

dilute their theological stance. He bravely affirmed that, 'As to those words *Antichrist*, found in our Liturgy, and *idolatry* and *deceit of Satan*, found in our Confession [of Faith], they be words declaring the grounds and reasons of our separation from the Romish Church, and doctrines which our fathers maintained in the worst of times, and which we are fully resolved as they, through the aids of Divine grace, never to abandon, but to keep faithfully and inviolably to the last gasp'.[1]

It is interesting to note that John Quick was writing his biography of Amyraut in 1696, eleven years after the Revocation of the Edict of Nantes (1685). Looking back wistfully, he wrote of the Synod of Loudun: 'I pray God, it may not be their last. It being six and thirty years since it was broken up [10 January 1660], and the churches in that kingdom are all ruined and desolate'.[2] The next synod was planned (DV) for Nîmes in 1662/3,[3] but it was never to be. However, according to the amazing providence of 'the wonderful Numberer',[4] and nine years after Quick's death, the next took place in the Cévennes in 1715, the very year Louis XIV died. But that is another and happier story![5]

It is appropriate here to mention that synods had a vital place in the life of the Reformed Churches of France. Respectful and courteous to both Anglican[6] and Roman Catholic churchmen, they remained committed to Reformed Faith and Order. Indeed, the Huguenots were as tenacious over their 'Order' as they were over their 'Faith'. Amyraut believed with Calvin and Beza that, according to clear New Testament teaching, 'elder' and 'bishop' were terms relating to one and the same individual,[7] as surely as 'elder' and 'deacon' denoted quite different roles.[8] He also taught that each church should be governed by a plural body or council of elders, that such a 'consistory'

---

1   Ibid. 513.
2   *Icones*, 999.
3   See Quick, *Synodicon*, ii. 582.
4   Ibid. i. p. clxiv.
5   See the account of Antoine Court in my *Calvin Celebrated: The Genevan Reformer & His Huguenot Sons* (Norwich: Charenton Reformed Publishing, 2009), 129ff.
6   Amyraut maintained friendly correspondence with Dr Cousins, future Bishop of Durham, whom he met in Paris. After the Restoration of Charles II, Amyraut congratulated his English friend. Quite unaware of the sufferings awaiting the Puritans at the Great Ejection of 1662, Amyraut dedicated his *Paraphrase on the Psalms* to the King (see Quick, *Icones*, 999, 1004).
7   See Titus 1:5–7.
8   See 1 Timothy 3:1–14.

was made up of 'Ministers of the Word' and 'ruling elders'.[1] Showing little sympathy for congregational independency, he also believed that synods had divine warrant.[2] They enabled churches to express connexional fellowship and solidarity. However, while French Reformed Church Order stated that provincial synods were to be 'subordinate' to national synods, it was only a 'self-subordination'. By referring to their 'churches' in plural terms, their approach was 'bottom-up' rather than 'top-down' as in the Presbyterian Church [singular] hierarchical system. Amyraut had already published a work on church order before the National Synod of Loudun.[3] At the Synod, he was commissioned to prepare a treatise showing the 'Conformity' of the discipline of the Reformed Churches of France with the 'ancient primitive Church'.[4] Dying before this work was finished, it was completed by his pupil Matthieu Larroque, Pastor of Quevilly near Rouen, whose treatise was later translated into English.[5]

As in England, where Anglicans regarded non-episcopally-ordained Puritans as not true ministers, so the French Roman Catholic clergy dismissed the orders of the Huguenot ministers. Ever concerned to combine courtesy with tenacity, Amyraut put his theory of church order to good use. When M. Péréfixe, Archbishop of Paris visited Saumur, he requested a meeting with Amyraut. Knowing the scriptural prohibition against bishops (= elders!) being 'lords' (*1 Peter 5:3*), Amyraut refused to address Roman Catholic bishops as 'My Lord' unless they were peers of the realm (itself an arrangement the Huguenots were hardly in a position to correct). Once the Archbishop—not being a peer—realised he would only be addressed as 'Mr', he agreed to an unofficial private meeting with Amyraut. While he was quite a civil man, he was possibly tinged with jealousy where the Parisian preacher Jean Daillé was concerned. Quick's revealing report is not without a touch of humour:

> They spent together in that conversation about three hours, discoursing of the affairs of the great world, and the most eminent persons for learning

---

1 See 1 Timothy 5:17.

2 See Acts 15.

3 See *Du gouvernement de l'eglise contre ceux qui veulent abolir l'usage & l'autorité des synodes* (Saumur: Isaac Desbordes, 1653; 2nd. ed. 1658, *Avec un appendice au livre du gouvernement de l'eglise où il est traité de la puissance des consistoires*.

4 *Icones*, 1001.

5 See *The Conformity of the Ecclesiastical Discipline of the Reformed Churches of France with that of the Primitive Christians* (London: 1691). For Larroque, see Quick, *Icone* 43.

and religion in the communion of both churches. This led them into a discourse of M. Daillé, a person of extraordinary parts and famous for his profound knowledge in the learned world. M. Amyraut observed that the Archbishop always spoke of him slightingly, and by the single name of Daillé; which made M. Amyraut never to mention him without a preface and title of honour.[1]

We have thus noticed that in those tense and potentially-explosive times, Amyraut was concerned to combine tenacity of conviction with courtesy and compassion. A beautiful example of the latter occurred in 1662, two years before he died. Following a bad harvest that year, there was a great shortage of corn in France.[2] Due to her wise management, Mme Amyraut had—Joseph-like—stocked up large reserves of corn at their country house in the Vale of Anjou. Says Quick, 'She had stacked it up in the barns and fields for sundry years of plenty together most abundantly'.[3] Urged to take financial advantage of the situation by selling the corn, the Amyrauts refused to follow what they construed as selfish and ungodly advice. Instead, while taking prudent care of his family and servants should bad harvests continue, they drew up a plan to distribute the corn freely to the poor, irrespective of religious persuasion. Observing Paul's directive to 'do good to all, especially to those who are of the household of faith' *(Galatians 6:10)*, first the Reformed poor, then the Roman Catholic poor benefited from their gracious generosity. Quick writes that 'the Roman Catholics whose hungry bellies and empty bowels were refreshed by him, loved and honoured him, calling him the common father of the poor, declaring that in his charities he made no distinction between them and those of his own religion'.[4]

At the commencement of the September vacation in 1663, the Amyrauts retired to their country house as usual. Within days Moïse became unwell, developing a high but intermittent fever. Instead of returning to Saumur for medical help, he stayed to enjoy a well-deserved rest. After several weeks, his condition deteriorating, Amyraut bowed to the inevitable and returned to

---

1   *Icones*, 1002–3. For further confirmation of Daillé's eminence, see Philip Benedict, *The Faith and Fortunes of France's Huguenots*, 254.
2   England's harvests were bad in the years 1658–61. See C. Hill, *The Century of Revolution, 1603–1714* (London: Nelson, 1961), 321.
3   *Icones*, 1005.
4   Ibid.

Saumur. Concern for his health grew and the sad news spread rapidly. Many anxious visitors called to see him, Roman Catholics as well as Reformed people. As his end drew near, he testified of his faith to a captive audience crowded around his bed. So moving were his last hours that Quick referred to Amyraut's death-bed utterances in a later funeral sermon. He did so to prove the dying man's fidelity to the Reformed Faith to the last:

> [He proved] the truth of the Christian religion, and of our Holy Reformed religion, by many unanswerable arguments. "This I have professed," said he; "I have preached this Holy Reformed religion well nigh forty years." And turning himself unto the Papists (for there were many then present in his chamber, spectators and witnesses of his last end) "Gentlemen," said he, "This is the only true religion, and out of it there is no salvation. That God to whom I am going knows that I do speak the very truth." This, and much more he uttered with a clear and audible voice; yea, and those very Papists heard him with much reverence and attention.[1]

He lingered several days, during which time many of his flock received their beloved pastor's final exhortations. Quick adds this further moving information:

> He had advised them to stand steadfast in the faith, and to hold fast to their profession without wavering, and to prepare against the evil times of sore trials which were approaching, for the God of judgement was at the door, and heavy judgements would begin at the house of God, and therefore how painful soever their cross and sufferings might be, they should not faint, nor prevaricate in, nor apostatise from their holy religion. For he protested to them in the presence of God to whose tribunal he was now a going, that it was the only true one in the whole world, and that out of it there was no salvation to be obtained. I say, after he had given them these and a great many other divine counsels, he blessed them in the name of the Lord'.[2]

The dying servant of God clearly foresaw the coming persecutions which afflicted the Reformed Churches of France two decades later. He had sufficient

---

1   *The Triumph of Faith* (London: 1698), 24.
2   *Icones*, 1007–8.

strength to repeat some of these exhortations to another pastor from Poitou who, passing through Saumur and hearing that Amyraut was dying, called to see him. Encouraging his rather diffident brother, Amyraut said: 'The doctrine I have taught my scholars in the university and my church in the city is the very truth of God, by which we must all be saved'.[1]

After giving his son directions about his will, Amyraut said farewell to his wife and family. Quick describes his last moments thus:

> In the fifteen last moments of his life, he joined his hands together, and lifted them up with his eyes unto heaven, waiting as dying Jacob did for God's salvation. And in that posture breathed out his blessed soul into the arms of his Redeemer'.[2]

And so this honoured servant of Christ died on the 18 January 1664, aged sixty-eight years. His dearly beloved wife, who also became ill during her husband's sickness, survived him by only a few months. Their son—whose own son Moses eventually settled here—met John Quick in London after escaping to England at the time of the Revocation of the Edict of Nantes. Quick describes him as a man 'of serious piety, being an illustrious confessor of our Lord Jesus in these woeful times of tribulation'.[3] He later served as an Advocate in the High Court of Justice in the Hague. After presenting an engraving of his father to one of the greatest of Amyraut's pupils, Pierre du Bosc[4]—Minister of the Reformed Church at Caen in Normandy and described by Louis XIV as the greatest orator in France—added to the

---

1   Ibid. 1009. Of course, this includes his 'doctrinal distinctives', and many continued to dispute Amyraut's claim. However, through the good offices of the Prince of Tarente, some reconciliation was achieved in 1649 (see Quick, *Icones*, 967). In 1655, even Pierre du Moulin responded positively to a conciliatory letter from Amyraut. His 'Amyraldian distinctives' were eventually regarded—at least by some former enemies—as 'innocent' and 'inoffensive' instead of 'shocking doctrine' (Quick, *Icones*, 1004; Bayle, 262). Sadly, subscribers to supra-scriptural Westminster orthodoxy think otherwise.
2   Ibid. 1010.
3   Ibid. 1012.
4   For Du Bosc (1623–92), see Quick *Icone* 47; Bayle, ii. 91. For academic life at Saumur, see J.-P. Pittion, 'Intellectual life in the Académie of Saumur, 1633–1685 (Unpublished PhD thesis, Trinity College, Dublin, 1970). This work is currently being prepared for publication. On a lighter note, Amyraut defended his young gentlemen against some dour critics of their high-spirited behaviour: "Our morose and supercilious critics had quite forgot that they had been also young lads" (*Icones*, 1016). Together with another student, Pierre du Bosc had been censured for his fashionable clothes!

portrait a personal Latin tribute to his professor. Thus translated, this worthy epitaph reads:

> From Moses down to Moses, none,
> Among the sons of men,
> With equal lustre ever shone,
> In manners, tongue and pen.[1]

Is it any wonder that Richard Baxter should be impressed by this man whose books he so much admired? Indeed, is it so dubious a privilege after all to be dubbed an Amyraldian?

---

[1] Bayle says these words were an allusion to what the Jews said in praise of their famous Rabbi Moses Maimonides [1135–1204]: 'A Mose ad Mosem par Mosi non fuit ullus: More, ore & calamo, mirus uterque fuit' (*Dictionary*, 265).

BRIEF
TRAITTE
DE LA
PREDESTINATION
ET DE SES PRINCIPA-
LES DEPENDANCES

Par **MOYSE AMYRAVT**
*Pasteur & Professeur en Theo-
logie à Saumur.*

A **SAVMVR**,
Par **IEAN LESNIER**, &
ISAAC DESBORDES.

M. DC. XXXIV.

Above: Title page of Amyraut's *Brief Treatise of Predestination*

DEFENSE DE LA DOCTRINE DE CALVIN.

SVR LE SVIET DE L ELECTION ET DE LA REPROBATION.

Par MOYSE AMYRAVT, *Pasteur & Professeur en Theologie a Saumur.*

A SAVMVR,
Chés ISAAC DESBORDES Imprimeur & Libraire, demeurant à l'Enseigne de l'Imprimerie.
M. DC. XLIV.

Above: Title page of Amyraut's *Defense of Calvin's doctrine on the subject of the election and reprobation*

Opposite above: Amyraut's *Treatise of Predestination* resting on Amyraut's chair.

Opposite below: Amyraut's place "at" Calvin's Table in the International Museum of the Reformation in Geneva, Switzerland (photos by A. C. Clifford).

Entrance to Saumur Academy where Amyraut would have walked (photo by A. C Clifford)

A Word About the Translation

Before one dives into Amyraut's text, it would be helpful to understand the nature and the scope of this translation from the language of Middle French to modern English.[1] Within literary production and translation theory, scholars such as Giles, Lederer, and Vinay define fidelity in translation as a premeditated attempt to understand thoroughly the original text not only at the level of syntax, argumentation, and diacritics, but also at the level of the author himself and the genesis of the meaning (sense) he is transmitting.[2] Thus, to understand the truest sense of any text, the translator must grasp the full intent of the author. Therefore, this personal sense to understand the life, ministry, and academic production of Moïse Amyraut has fueled this unique translation into modern English of his original *Brief Treatise*. From the outset of this translation project, I have endeavored to master the life and communication of Amyraut in his literary production, the seventeenth century French language he employed in the process, and the mindset of the potential present day audience who would be newly introduced to Amyraut's unique theological methodology concerning the doctrine of predestination from this modern English translation. As such, I have undertaken the opportunity to render a critical translation to a contemporary audience of Amyraut's unique and infamous *Brief Treatise*, the very purpose of which has been to deliver with all equanimity Amyraut's full intention as expressed through his own words. Because Amyraut's treatise has heretofore never been read in a critically translated published English work, it is my hope to present with all

---

1 Middle French (*moyen français*) is a historical division of the French language that covers the period from the 14th to the early 17th centuries.
2 See Daniel Giles, "Fidélité et Litéralité Dans la Traduction: Une Approche Pédagogique," in *Babel* 28, 1982; Marianne Lederer, *La Traduction Aujourd'hui: Le Modèle Interpretatif* (Vanves: France: Hachette, 1994); Hans Schulte and Gerhart Teuscher, eds. *The Art of Literary Translation* (New York: Universal Press of America, 1993); and J.Vinay and J. Darbelnet, *Stylistique Comparée du Français et de L'Anglais* (Paris: Didier, 1958).

fidelity Amyraut's own passion, intention, and theological skill in this text as never before read in modern English.

As mentioned in the introduction, the paucity of original manuscripts of Amyraut's *Brief Treatise* (1634) is remarkable with only a few extant first edition copies remaining in the world. However, recent scholarship and the advancement of technology have now enabled one of those copies to be digitally reproduced and placed permanently online for instant perusal.[1] However, Amyraut's original treatise is written in early seventeenth century French and the typeset, ink, and paper within these copies have been naturally degraded over the years, making a clean and easily reproducible copy almost impossible. More so, many words and phrases within these original copies have been marred by almost four hundred years of wear on the copy itself, making the accurate reconstruction a veritable challenge. Therefore, I traveled to several countries within Europe and within the United States to compare various extant copies of the first edition *in toto* in order to verify and authenticate (1) first that each of the alleged original copies was exactly the same, and (2) second, where in some copies there was significant deterioration, the translator could reconstruct an accurate text in question by use of these other copies.[2] I took the same steps with Amyraut's only other edition of the *Brief Treatise* (1658).[3] Having compared and validated that the first edition text was completely preserved among the collation of

---

[1] For a complete description of where each of these original editions are found, see Nicole, "Moyse Amyraut,"156–157. For the online version of the original 1634 edition in French, see Moïse Amyraut, *Brief Treatise of Predestination* (1634) at Google Books at http://tinyurl.com/hbk8xxv.

[2] Having permission from the Bibliotèque Nationale de Paris and the Bibliotèque de la Société de l'Histoire de Protestantisme Français who each have one extant copy of Amyraut's first edition (1634) text, compared with copies in both Princeton Seminary and Reformed Theological Seminary in Orlando, the author had the ability to cross-reference all four first edition texts and verify that there are no variances between them. Further, in comparing the texts of the same edition and printing, the author was able to substantiate that each text was indeed printed from the same printing press in Saumur, France from printers Jean Lesnier and Isaac Desbordes. Having compared these texts, the author then traveled to the Bodleian Library at Oxford University in Oxford, England and inspected their only copy of the first edition (1634) as well. Upon completion of the inspection of the texts, the author validated that a digital copy which was produced by Princeton University (2004) was in fact one and the same as the five extant copies in Europe, England, and the United States.

[3] The same process applied to Amyraut's second (1658) edition of the *Brief Traité* whereby I validated that the extant copies in Europe and at Harvard University were equivalent and that a baseline copy could be established from which to translate and compare the texts. Once each

six extant copies, it was determined that Amyraut's text in full was available to translate into modern English.

The Text

The first edition text of Amyraut's *Brief Treatise* (1634) was written in the common early-modern French (or in the "common tongue") rather than in the technical, academic, or philosophical Latin as would be expected of a theological treatise in Amyraut's day. The literary age when Amyraut penned his treatise was in the middle of a major linguistic change within France.[1] Having just changed the official language of the French royal court from Latin to French (Middle French) less than one hundred years prior to Amyraut's life and writing, Amyraut produced his theological prose in a fertile few decades where pastors, along with authors of all disciplines, would help shape the tenor of the French language.[2] As such, notwithstanding the various linguistic changes between the first (1634) and second (1658) editions of the *Brief Treatise*, Amyraut's late Middle-French or Early Modern French, depending on the subscribed classification taxonomy, presents a rather robust challenge to the modern translator since the language and attached meanings

---

edition was verified as original to that edition, the author proceeded to analyze the text itself, the language, and ultimately the argument which Amyraut advances within his work.

1 The one hundred years between 1534 and 1634, the year of Amyraut's publishing of the *Brief Treatise*, was momentous for the French language. In 1539, the French language became official through royal decree and since has taken on a rich linguistic heritage all its own. At the end of the sixteenth century, Middle French began to evolve into early-modern French and the foundation of the Académie Française (French Academy) in 1634 by Cardinal Richelieu sealed the language's notoriety and purposed development, since the academy's official role has been the purification and preservation of the French language. Following a period of unification, regulation, and purification (latinisation), the early-modern French of the 17th and 18th centuries is also called Classical French (*Français Classique*), of which pastors and popular authors helped shape through speaking and writing sermons and treatises. For more insight into the evolution of early-modern French, see R. Anthony Lodge, *French: From Dialect to Standard* (New York: Routledge, 1993) and Bernard Cerquiglini, *La Naissance du Français*, 2 ed. (Paris: Presses Universitaires de France, 1993).

2 In league with the first ever French dictionary being published in 1539, King Francis I of France made French the official language of his royal administration and court proceedings in France, rejecting Latin that had been used for over seven hundred years prior. Rejecting the Latin declension system, the first French dialect is called Middle French (*moyen français*) as described by the first grammatical description of French in Louis Maigret, *Tretté de la Grammaire Française* (Paris: Weebel, 1550).

themselves have so variably changed through time, culture, and genre in almost four hundred years of usage, development, and natural linguistical evolution.[1]

Linguist Peter Rickard notes the unique difficulty for the modern translator in producing an accurate translation with fidelity to the original with such cultural and linguistical gaps present. He remarks, "It does not follow that the modern editor knows more than seventeenth-century Frenchmen did about their own language; he cannot share their experience of it, save through a glass darkly; he cannot *live* it as they did; and their vocabulary (for instance) had overtones and associations which are only partially available to us today, or not at all."[2] However, and particularly so with Amyraut, his writing style and choice of syntax seem rather problematic and at times confusing even when compared to his contemporaries' writings throughout France. Brian Armstrong, one of the few who have attempted to translate Amyraut's work into modern English, concludes that Amyraut's literary technique contains "a heavy style, annoyingly cluttered with appositional phrases."[3] Amyraut's French in this treatise is verbose, at times lumbering, and filled with expressive, yet by modern grammatical standards, run-on sentences throughout.[4] Within his "brief" treatise of 196 Quarto pages, Amyraut took many linguistical liberties in his mode of expression and illustration. Typically, Amyraut would cite at least two or three examples of each point and sub-point he was making. More so, in the middle of his sentences where he would both build an argument and provide warrants validating his claims, Amyraut would characteristically insert several descriptive clauses as referents to his main nouns or as further elucidation of his point. Thus, both in reading and translating such a thick and cumbersome style of prose, reproducing Amyraut's treatise into modern

---

1 Rickard states, "A consensus would place either at the end of the sixteenth century, or in the early decades of the seventeenth, the end of the Middle French period and the emergence, in its essentials, of a form of the language clearly recognizable as Modern French." Peter Rickard, *The French Language in the Seventeenth Century* (New York: D.S. Brewer, 1992), 3.

2 Rickard, *The French Language*, vii. Italics original to Rickard.

3 Brian G. Armstrong, *Calvinism and the Amyraut Heresy* (Eugene, OR: Wipf & Stock), 73.

4 A typical example of one of Amyraut's run-on sentences would take up one whole side of a page and simply contain a random comma in unexpected places. An example is as follows: "For example, if a rich treasure is presented to a man who is pressed by necessity, or a beneficial medication to someone who is mortally ill, the one could not have a true knowledge of his poverty and of the quality of the treasure which had been given to him, nor could the other have the true knowledge of his sickness, of the peril in which he is and of the virtue of the medication which is secured for him in it, if he is not immediately impelled to receive it ..." Amyraut, *Brief Treatise*, 141.

English with the aim of being most faithful to his words, thought, and creative expression proved an arduous task.

For this translation project, I have attempted to render a more literal and word for word translation where sensible. For much of the treatise, it was possible to translate each word or phrase literally, capturing Amyraut's intention, while also attempting to produce a similar reading comparable to a seventeenth century French audience. Amyraut kept idiomatic expressions to a minimum, choosing rather to explain his various arguments by common illustrations relatable to his audience comprised of farmers, mechanics, tradesmen, fishermen, and soldiers. As such, if idiomatic expressions were employed by Amyraut, a suitable equivalent based on his particular argument or illustration was chosen with correspondence to his usage. However, where the more literal delivery is demanded from the text, translating word for word, the strictly literal rendition accounts sometimes for a more clumsy English translation, even when smoothed out for clarity. The one exception is demonstrated in the titles of each chapter. Rather than translating each title exactly or literally, the titles have been modernized for efficiency and clarity of thought, yet without losing any of the context or meaning. Further, where any French words or phrases have needed to remain in the English translation, in the body or within the footnotes, the translator has kept the exact phrasing of Amyraut's Middle French without accent marks, modernization, or any change to its original orthography. Similarly, where Amyraut highlights a word or accentuates a phrase in his original text, so the translation follows suit.

Since the goal of fidelity in translation is the passing of the message from one language into another by producing the same effect in the other language, in both sense and form, and in a way that the reader of the translation would react exactly as the reader of the original text, the more literal the translation, the more accurate representation of the original thought and intent. Therefore, attempting to stay true to Amyraut's intended words and particular thought within this English translation, there has been little periphrastic license taken, if only in word choice and diacritical placement.

At times where certain words in Middle French have abated, a more dynamic equivalency (thought for thought) was employed. For example, the word "emotion" was substituted throughout the treatise in context of man's tri-part constitution for the French word *affections*, since the import of the

French word *affections* was attenuated in the nineteenth century.[1] Another example would be the dynamic translation of the French phrase, "*un effect vulgaire*," which has no modern counterpart in English. Thus, the phrase "a common result" was employed.[2] Where unique words are found throughout the treatise, either being theologically significant or linguistically peculiar, they have been indicated in the explanatory notes below the text. For example, relating to a significant theological concept throughout the treatise, the French word *arrest* was varyingly translated as either decree, judgment, or ordinance, even though modern French has dropped all theological and judicial meaning in the French word *arrêt* which now simply means "stop" or "arrest."[3]

In addition to adding dynamic equivalent thoughts where a literal translation was not possible, I also changed punctuation and paragraph indentions where necessary. Amyraut seemingly follows the normal usage of punctuation for his time, where semi-colons act more like commas and colons are placed at the end of sentences to represent varyingly a stop in the words, but not of the thought being communicated. Sometimes, the punctuation makes little sense to the modern observer, which may be the result of a rushed printer's typeset or it may simply be intended. For example, here is a small section of Amyraut's original edition demonstrating unique punctuation:

> Il faloit que le premier home ayant esté pris de la terre eust des conditions terriennes sortables à son origine, c'est à dire corruptibles etmuables, comme sont toutes les choses qui ont esté pris de la matiere des elemens; auparavant que le second Adam descendist des cieux, à qui seul comme a un principe surnaturel et celeste, appartenoit de communiquer à ceux qui auroyent communion avec luy, des conditions celestes et incorruptibles Que si Dieu n'eust pas voulu mettre l'homme en un estat tout à fait surnaturel et immutable, et neantmoins luy fournir aux occasions la force qui luy eust esté necessaire pour empecher que ce qui pouvoit arriver,

---

[1] *Affections* translated as "emotion." See p.156 in the original or p. 139 in the translation. For example, the word *demonstration* has been variously translated as "proof." See p. 139 in the original or p. 130 in the translation.

[2] *Un Effect Vulgaire* translated as "a common result." See p. 145 in the original or p. 132.

[3] *Arrest* translated as "decree." See p. 124 in the original or p. 123 in the translation. Another example is the phrase "*Une estoitte communion de sang*" which today could be translated as "a human bond." See p. 123 in the original or p. 123 in the translation.

c'est à sçavoir, sa mutation, n'arrivast, et le render impenetrable aux traicts du malin; toujours ...[1]

It is possible that where the beginning of the capitalized Q in *Que* or [that] is placed is supposed to mark the start of a new sentence, yet the random placement of the semi-colons throughout do not lend the right break in thoughts as punctuated. Thus, where appropriate, I have added needful punctuation in the form of commas, semi-colons, em dashes, and colons where not originally found in Amyraut's text. Typically where Amyraut adds parenthetical statements in the middle of his sentences, the translator has replaced them with either commas if possible and em dashes where the break in thought is too significant.

Though one could easily follow the logical progression of thought in Amyraut's chapter delineation, his paragraph demarcations within each chapter are rather protracted and, at times, perplexing. Amyraut's normal paragraph breaks can sometimes extend over several pages. When Amyraut sets out to explain and illustrate a principle point, it may take him several pages of an unbroken paragraph to communicate what he thinks is one complete thought. Therefore, in comparable fashion, the English translation mirrors abnormally long paragraphs more accurate to Amyraut's style. However, as much as was needed, new paragraph breaks were introduced in order to set off new ideas and arguments and allow the previous statements to stand alone with more prominence. As such, the additional punctuation introduced allows the English translation to read more smoothly and the additional paragraph breaks ease the flow of Amyraut's arguments so that the detailed ideas specific to each paragraph can stand on their own.

AMYRAUT'S MARGINALIA

Within Amyraut's *Brief Treatise*, he adds Scripture references within the margin of his text, citing chapter and verse and sometimes directing his readers to note various verses associated with his biblical points. With over one hundred and forty verses quoted throughout his entire treatise, Amyraut makes a point to help his readers both know the Scripture quoted and where their biblical references are to be found in the Bible. Further, where Amyraut italicizes

---

[1] Amyraut, *Brief Treatise*, 44–45. This sentence goes on five more lines before a period is ever introduced. With fourteen lines in all, this paragraph could count as one long run-on sentence.

the Scripture verse within his text, so the English translation also denotes each Scripture within the body of the work through italics. However, in the English translation, I have moved each overt scriptural citation from the margin as found in the original and placed them either at the end of the verse itself, parenthetically within the text, or to the footnotes if Amyraut was only alluding to a biblical verse or passage. Where indicated in the original text, the translator has placed the actual scriptural reference parenthetically in mid-sentence and only where Amyraut attempted to introduce Scripture into his own main sentence structure. In a few places, Amyraut quoted Scripture without adding the citation. In these instances, the translator has added the appropriate citations within the text in uniform fashion. Thus, wherever Amyraut directs supplementary information in his margins, these have each been cited within the footnotes in the English translation.

Further, Amyraut strictly employed abbreviations (such as 1 Pet. 3:11) for his scriptural citations within the margin. However, where the verses appear in the translation either in the text itself or within a footnote, the complete biblical reference has been spelled out (such as 1 Peter 3:11). Last, for easier reference and citation, I have added the original pagination numbering in brackets (such as [172]) within the text to indicate where in the translation the original paragraph breaks may be found in the first edition (1634). Each of these paginated brackets have been placed at the beginning of each paragraph.

Explanatory Notes

Within this new modern English translation I have also introduced explanatory notes pertinent to either the text itself, commentary about the immediate context, or concerning Amyraut's greater theology within footnotes. I have employed the explanatory notes to designate significant additions pertinent to the original text either theologically, historically, or syntactically by way of linguistic explanation. In addition to providing references, explaining allusions, evaluating the ideas and opinions expressed by Amyraut, and weighing his methodology as critically as possible given the distance in time, culture, and language, the explanatory notes also help to outline various critical claims and statements made throughout the treatise.

The first use of the explanatory notes concerns citing Scripture verses which Amyraut intended for his readers. For this translation, where Amyraut specifically cites a verse, I have left that Scripture in the body of the text and signaled its use by adding parentheses. When Amyraut simply references Scripture without actually quoting it, I have denoted such through footnotes with the abbreviation Cf. Second, throughout the treatise, I have introduced various observations explaining either the history surrounding the controversy which Amyraut perpetuated through this very treatise or commentary explaining more clearly some of Amyraut's arguments. Third, where there are certain phrases which need to be glossed or reinterpreted thought for thought, I have denoted such within the footnotes for clarification. At times, where unique words or phrases are employed by Amyraut, those are also indicated within the notes, sometime with the subsequent translation, but mostly without. The explanatory notes are intended to be a critical tool for any necessary explanation or citation which is germane to Amyraut's main argument. I have used the explanatory notes sparingly, hoping to encourage the reader to ponder, without excessive guidance, Amyraut's original arguments and explanation in his own words.

Last, on the seventh page of the introductory matter within Amyraut's original *Brief Treatise* (1634) edition, Amyraut lists five typological errors to be corrected (*fautes à corriger*). These five noted errors were corrected in the translation as they had also been corrected in the (1658) edition.

Conclusion

Faced with the challenge of making metaphors, analogies, and idioms understandable to a new audience for English speakers, the following translation has also attempted to capture Amyraut's unique tone, inflection, theological quality, and the other intangible elements of his written word in order to convey those critical ideas meaningfully to a new audience. Therefore, attempting to minimize various literary or cultural ambiguities, including minimizing where possible Amyraut's more verbose style, I have endeavored to be technically accurate with all fidelity to Amyraut's words, phrases, and figures of speech which he passionately communicated to his audience nearly four hundred years ago. Because Amyraut's words had real meaning in the seventeenth century to his readership, so his words too can live on today reaching a new audience with his engaging theological method toward a more comprehensible perspective of the doctrine of predestination. The following modern English translation is presented as an honorable effort toward literary and theological faithfulness to Amyraut's unique covenantal understanding and explanation of predestination and Christ's universal atonement. Thanks must be rendered to Brian G. Armstrong and Richard Lum who both attempted in part a translation of the *Brief Treatise* (1634) with the limited source material available to them in the nineteen sixties and nineteen eighties respectively. Thanks also is necessary to Alan Clifford for his tireless efforts in all causes "Amyraldian" over the last many decades. Clifford's brief survey of Amyraut's life and context within this book is unsurpassed.

A BRIEF TREATISE CONCERNING PREDESTINATION AND ITS DEPENDENT PRINCIPLES

By Moïse Amyraut

Pastor and Professor of Theology at Saumur

Published in Saumur, France by Jean Lesnier and Isaac Desbordes, 1634

Introduction

To the reader: The reasons which led me not so long ago to write this little treatise concerning predestination have also required that it be very brief and permit that I write only in the fashion and language of the people. Hence, there is no point in seeking truly profound speculations of the type which were produced in those schools when subject matter like the present is discussed. My intention has solely been to render this doctrine that is commonly evaluated to be both difficult and problematic (thorny) as capable to be understood by all and to take it back from the subtlety of the controversy, where too often passion negatively taints the mind and prejudices of the partisans which also hinders the capacity for (1) true understanding, (2) the practice of piety, and (3) the edification and consolation of the conscience. Herein, I have only dealt with those subjects which are especially erroneous and have prevented the desired outcome of clarity. Further, I know that the present subject is so imposing[1] that it would take more dexterity than I possess to truly render it easily grasped by each person. Nevertheless, I think I have offered this discussion in such a manner that those who will pay as much attention to the reading of this booklet as they do to the least important subjects of no comparison, they will find here specifically that which can encourage their heart. As for those who neglect that which is their instruction in religion, or those who only apply it by way of passive acknowledgement—so great was that production and the sufficiency that another had taken on—for these it would have been useless. For even the light of the sun is only seen by those who open their eyes. Those who neglectfully always keep their eyes closed, or those who deliberately blind themselves (and it happens only too often in matters of religion that men voluntarily blind themselves to true meaning) should by necessity live out their days in darkness, though they were surrounded everywhere by the brightest light. I have, therefore, wanted to inform the reader of my full

---

1   *De foi si haute* ... lit. "of such high faith or belief."

intention from the very beginning, so that no one will be taken back that in this brief writing the author only deals with subjects within the limits of the immediate purpose, which is the nature of predestination.

TABLE OF CONTENTS

1. What is Predestination?   57
2. Why God Created the World in General   63
3. Why God Created Mankind in Particular   69
4. Why God Permitted The First Man to Sin   73
5. What Are the Consequences of the First Man's Sin   83
6. What Was God's Design in Sending His Son to the World   91
7. What Is the Nature of the Decree by Which God Ordained to Accomplish this Design: Its Extent, Or the Condition of Faith upon Which It Depends   99
8. What Is Sinful Man's Inability to Accomplish His Own Salvation   107
9. The Election and Predestination of God by which He has Ordained to accomplish Salvation in Some and Not in Others: Why Does This Occur?   113
10. That According to This Doctrine God Cannot Be Accused of Being a "Respecter of Persons," or of Being the Author of Sin, or the Cause of Man's Damnation   121
11. How One Discerns the Means by Which God Accomplishes This Condition of Faith in His Elect and Renders His Predestination as a Certain and Infallible Reality   127
12. That in the Process of Predestination God Does Not Destroy Man's Free Will   135

13. That this Doctrine of Predestination Does Not Lead to Spiritual Apathy Nor Extinguishes Concern for Holy Living, But Invokes the Opposite   143

14. That This Doctrine Fills the Conscience of the Faithful with Joy and Consolation.   153

Chapter I

What is Predestination?

[1]¹ Concerning the causes which one commonly refers to as *natural*, such as the sky and earthly elements, these carry on for an unseen and preordained² necessity; the beasts of the earth are led to act by instinct and raw appetites which are unto themselves unknown, while those endowed with intelligence such as angels and men are driven by a more excellent faculty and are capable of self-reflection and understanding the motives of their actions, ultimately being able to carry out their own intended desires. In the manner which men busy themselves with fine art, research, and scientific knowledge, attending to government, or to religion and virtue, or be they even of matters of the least importance regardless of their nature, if these are not children or insane, or men otherwise hindered in their understanding, these persons know why they give themselves to such matters and are able to give some rational explanation for the goal set before them. Moreover, it is true that within the condition to which men live, they are subjected to many passions and evil lusts which maintain a strong force over their reason, such that it happens rather often that even for a similar action two men will have two marvelously different goals, each governed by his own passion. And then there are those in whom alone these affections are purified and steadied in reason, which even in the good and praiseworthy actions of these anticipate a praiseworthy and worthwhile end.

[2] Moreover, an intelligent nature is permeated with virtue and is free from corrupting sins,³ its goal being unquestionably to become more excellent

---

1 The numbered brackets at the beginning of each paragraph indicate the original numbered Quarto pages of Amyraut's 1634 edition of the *Brief Treatise*.
2 Inevitable or unavoidable.
3 Desires.

to which it conforms all its action. Yet whether good or bad, there is always some end chosen by our intelligence upon which, whatever we do, we have our design. If, therefore, we would not be informed of it elsewhere, and had the Holy Spirit not so clearly taught it in the Word, nature itself would teach us that God is an intelligent being, Himself being the very source from which follows all reason in his creature. Thus, God does not act out at random or at lost causes, but He necessarily acts with purpose and a goal in mind. And since all the universe comprises His work and all the parts it contains where He maintains it,[1] being firmly in His hands whether great or small, high or low, vile or precious, loathsome or honorable, whether good or evil—it is necessary that within their very creation and in their composition, together with their care and composition, and within their administration and conduct, God has certain ends to which He has destined them all. Similarly, as it would be absurd to imagine an architect not having had a formal design for the structure of a building in which can be detected a perfectly good blueprint of the proportions and measurements, of the material and their proper use and of their positioning and connections, thus, in the same way it would be an unworthy conception of the beauty which appears in the constitution of the world and of the knowledge[2] of the One who formed it, thinking this universe could have been created on the fly without having particularly determined each reality with a specific purpose. And since God is nowhere subject to the passions which dominate man, being that the principle of holy light and virtue resides in His eternal Person—of which we see of His grace a few rays shining here and there within the best of men—it is impossible that the design to which these actions tend not to be the most exquisite of all, or suitable to the incomparable purity of this holy being who oversees it. Seen principally with this marvelous holiness, there is conjoined in Him an infinite and incomprehensible wisdom.

[5] Further, as is proper of intelligent persons not to neglect those things which contribute to their own design, and however to have a particular respect to those things which shine some excellence over others and appropriate them to their design[3] and use which agrees with them—such would be similar to placing the carefully shaped marble, the gold, the colors and oil

---

1 "... . parts, either those that compose it or those contained in it."
2 Wisdom.
3 Design or end. In the Middle French *but* or *fin*.

paintings in the foundation of the building and in turn placing the foundation rubble as clearly visible in the front of the house—is it not necessary to revoke doubt that God had not given particular care to His creatures by giving them the upper hand of having wisdom and being able to excel in a variety of ways? So that man is the masterpiece of His hand and the abstract of wonders which He has here and there variously distributed among all of His works, it is evident that His care must be engaged toward those things which concern Him, particularly in leading man to a certain purpose fitting to the condition of his nature. Thus, man is man! That is, that among all other creatures within creation, man alone displays reason and his principal excellence comprises the perfection of his understanding and affections which depend on it. Further, this perfection lies in the knowledge and love of things which he owes to his Creator and fellow men, and consequently, is an exceptionally remarkable quality in itself which represents the very nature of God. Therefore, not only the wisdom of the creator which requires that everything be suitably arranged, but even his goodness and love which he brings to all who hold fast to him and reflect him, will cause his gaze to focus upon this most precious piece of the universe, in order to establish an eternally blessed end[1] which transcends the end to which other creatures are ordained, just as man's understanding and will transcend all other faculties, and his piety and virtue surpass even the perfection of which these other creatures are beautified.

[7] At present, this description is what one normally refers to as "Predestination." Truthfully, if one only holds to the general meaning of the word, it is more universally understood as "Providence;" this signifies the care of God, the Creator of the universe, employing His wisdom, preservation, and the guidance of all things which make up the world. In this manner, apart from God, nothing happens on the earth—be it the things which appear to depend on nature, such as the influences of the heavens or the mixing of the elements in the composition of things, or the production (generation) of animals for the propagation of their species and similar processes, be it in the things which happen "by chance" of which at times there appears to be no perceivable cause in the order of nature, be it even in the actions of men—nothing happens on earth except what God has ordained by His own counsel. Appropriately, the Psalmist states, "*Our God is in heaven; He*

---

1 "... in order to destine it for an end."

does whatever pleases him" (Psalms 115:3).[1] And the Apostle Paul states, *"In Him, we have also obtained an inheritance, having been predestined according to His purpose who works all things after the counsel of His will"* (Ephesians 1:11). Truly, then, this word "Predestination" is used at times in Scripture in the more general meaning of providence. Another example is Saint Peter stating that the enemies of Jesus *"were anointed ... to do whatever Your hand and Your purpose destined to occur"* (Acts 4:28). However, since the word "providence" is more often employed as that process which generally oversees the direction of the world, predestination is understood rather to apply not only to the act of providence which universally watches over the actions of men, but particularly guides (each action) according to which God has ordained their very end. This is the sense in which Saint Paul says that those whom God has foreknown, *"He also predestined to become conformed to the image of His Son ... and those whom He predestined, He called"* (Romans 8:29–30). Elsewhere Saint Paul states, *"we have obtained an inheritance having been predestined according to His purpose"* (Ephesians 1:11). Further, *"He predestined us to adoptions as sons through Jesus Christ"* (Ephesians 1:5), this adoption therefore signifies that we are to *"become conformed to the image of His Son"* (Romans 8:29).

[9] However, between the first creation of mankind and his end to which the Apostle Paul stated we have been ordained—that is to be adopted and conformed in Jesus Christ—sin intruded of which the effects and fallout have been dreadful in the entire world; sin seems to have changed not only the face of the universe but even the design of His first creation—if we may speak this way—and prompted God to take counsel within Himself.[2] In order to

---

1   In this treatise, Amyraut employs direct quotes from Scripture and at times his own paraphrasing with emphasis. In this translation, I have sought to maintain Amyraut's emphasis between the two, both paraphrasing and rendering direct quotes of Scripture taken from the *The Holy Bible: New International Version* (Grand Rapids, MI: Zondervan, 1984).

2   "... *induit Dieu à prendre de nouveaux conseils.*" The literal verbage "induces God to take new counsels" was highly irregular for traditional 17th century Reformed usage. Though Amyraut did not change or "correct" this type of language here in his second edition (1658), the language which described the sovereign God as changing any of His counsels or decrees whatsoever was extremely offensive to the Reformed orthodoxy of his day since they explained (within their supralapsarian framework) God as having immutably decreed predestination in eternity past without any possibility of changing or modifying creation, the fall, or man's repentance. The interchangeability between the words "counsels" and "decrees" within Amyraut's writing also led to further confusion for the orthodox, since Amyraut used them in connection with the duality of God's own nature and will (both conditional and absolute wills within God). However, Amyraut admits to employing certain

disentangle correctly the most important complications which seem to occur in this manner because of the forced changes in man's sinful nature and his dependents,[1] one must consider these things separately, one after the other, and to speak first of the general sense of which the world had been ordained in general (general predestination) before tackling particularly the ordination of man in specific predestination, thus, pursuing each matter in its order.

---

anthropomorphisms within his treatise, such as the divine "counsel," as a method of accommodation to soften and clarify difficult concepts within the nature of predestination. Here and throughout the treatise, Amyraut employs the softer term "counsel" concerning God's malleable intention (purpose) within predestination which he later called God's conditional, revealed, and universal will; concerning the counsel of God's action within predestination that is fixed (unchangeable), Amyraut concurrently labeled it as God's absolute, hidden, and particular will. Embracing a paradoxical duality within God's will, Amyraut held that Scripture more easily identified God as both willing salvation universally while particularly electing men through saving faith.

1 "*& en ses dependances.*" Alternatively, "and its implications."

CHAPTER 2

WHY GOD CREATED THE WORLD IN GENERAL[1]

[10]   If it was a question of giving a good reason for why God formed each part of the earth in the way we see it and brought everything together in this perfect order, it would simply be a matter of appealing to God's wisdom. Because God created the sun to illuminate the universe, He put the earth in the middle as the lowest spot and created the earth to hold the weightiness of all matter so that animals would have a home in which to roam; He scattered the oceans to their assigned places where they would receive the waters of the earth, so as to avoid flooding throughout all lands, and act as a channel of commerce and communication of nations far removed for each other. The same is true of every other piece perfectly placed within this great home called earth. Yet, in consideration of the purpose of all this order, one must establish a more universal cause.[2]

Concerning the purpose of all this, one must consider both the Worker and the work. As does happen sometimes, the common use of the work is different in principal than the purpose for which it was proposed. For example, the purpose of the watch is to mark the division of the day into that which we call hours and the function of a man's house is for a man's habitation; yet it is possible that the watchmaker had grander intentions than its common functions, that is to say perhaps he designed the watch for his own enjoyment or for profit, and the architect of a house for the same

---

1   In this second chapter, Amyraut employs his inductive logic from creation and from divine providence that God, since He a God of both order and caring providence, is ultimately trustworthy with each individual's life, having created a beneficial beginning for each being, a useful (functional) life, and a purposed end—all for His glory. Amyraut will employ this argument later in the treatise to demonstrate that God is trustworthy even in the mystery of predestination, even when His hidden will demands faith for each individual to respond rightly to God.

2   Purpose.

reasons. We must investigate here within the function of the world to see if it is not the same reality.

[11] Of course the natural purpose of the world can only be the reflection of glory to the One who made it. By design God has given to the universe itself some concept of its being and of the marvelously beautiful composition of its many parts, and to each of those parts He has given some knowledge of the obligation of its existence to its Creator; thus, one must not doubt that all of the parts of creation, in general and in particular, have united toward the celebration of those virtues which God has instilled within them: His power in creating them; His wisdom in the order that He has kept in them; and His goodness which has led them to testify as such. Therefore, we say that the natural function of the watch is to keep time, by the force of its springs and the movement of its wheels and the general arrangement of all its parts which compose the watch, all these parts are working together toward this goal. Similarly, the purpose of a house is habitation by man since its walls, its roof, and its boards contribute together to this use. Thus, concerning the universal agreement which would arise for all creatures to the glory of their Creator, if they had an understanding of the virtues which He has displayed in them, we would conclude that in this lies their natural purpose. And this is the Prophet's meaning when he says that *"the heavens declare the glory of the mighty God, and the firmament gives testimony of His handiwork. As one day breaks forth in words to the next, and one night demonstrates knowledge to another night. There is no language in them and no speech, and yet their voice is heard continually"* (Psalms 19:1–2). Therefore, he says that such sorts of creatures, being destitute of intelligence and of sensible organs by means of which rational natures can express their understanding, these creatures are not able by themselves to proclaim truly the glory of the One who formed them, yet God has imprinted upon them marks of His above mentioned virtues, which show themselves to be so illustrious in every way that they are for them a kind of language through which they do proclaim it and invite all other creatures who can to recognize it. In this they signify sufficiently that if God had given them understanding as well as existence, their continual occupation would be the commemoration of His glory, and this would be their duty and without doubt their most natural purpose. Thus, one recalls the highly quoted phrase that "God has created everything for His glory," understanding that God indeed created all things for Himself, the very duty of these creatures and consequently their very purpose, being to serve Him.

[13] Nevertheless, if we focus more expressly toward the purpose for which God has precisely and particularly anticipated in the very creation of the world, it appears that His purpose seems different from the present reality than what is seen (understood) within the world. That does not mean that God sought His own profit for this creation like the artists do in the majority of their works. Rather, He possesses within Himself for all eternity all treasures and could acquire nothing within this universe or the works of creation that could somehow contribute to His contentment. Nor has God intended this universe to serve as some object of amusement like that found in the braggarts who are self-pleased with their invention, or the excellent painters who stare at their canvases admiring their work more by the minute than before, becoming even smitten within their own industry.

For God knew from all eternity the virtues which are already in Him before He gave any proof of these in the production of things. And if He takes contentment in the recognition of His admirable properties—in reality, as love is always accompanied by kindness and by pleasure, His virtues cannot be such that He does not love them completely nor consequently without unspeakable contentment—He could not love Himself more after the creation of the world than before, since neither are His virtues augmented nor His recognition of them. But since God is without question a supremely perfect essence and beyond the comprehension of our understanding, He must have had before his eyes the most excellent purpose that His actions could have had and that which was in closest agreement with the perfection of His nature.

[14] And it seems that He has imprinted upon the spirits of men a mark of what that purpose was. For certainly, the human actions which merit the most praise are those which arise transparently for virtue. And although virtuous actions naturally merit praise either as a necessary corollary or as a splendor arising for the beauty of the virtue, it is evident that the purpose of virtuous men in their actions should not properly be to their own praise, but rather the exercise of virtue for its own sake. Concerning the virtues of praise and glory—having a beauty which is merely borrowed from the splendor of the virtue from which they arise and virtue itself being a beautiful and luminous thing by itself which does not derive its commendation from elsewhere—these virtues are lovable in themselves in contrast to the others which are only lovable because of their source and principle. On the one hand a virtuous man does not refuse the praise that is given to him for the virtuous actions which he has performed, and even finds it strange and evil

when such praise is not given (for where it arises that each is so careful about his own reputation), if when he performed them he did not have as his principle purpose to be praised, but did this thing which merited praise afterwards either principally or solely in view of its own excellence and because it was in this that his duty and the perfection of these faculties and of his being consisted. Conversely, if anyone, as often happens due to the corruption of our spirits, has more regard for the glory than for the virtue itself, as do the hypocritical and the ambitious, he lessens the praise-worthiness of his actions to the extent that in it he has had envy and desire for praise. If therefore all the things which are beautiful and praiseworthy in men are merely flickers and reflections of those which are supremely beautiful and praiseworthy in God, the principle end to which God would have aimed in the creation of the world, considering it precisely, would not have been so much His own glory as the exercise of His virtues from which as we have said above His glory inescapably produces.[1]

[17] Emphatically, then, this next point is surpassingly important, being that the foremost of God's virtues which appear in the creation of the world is his *goodness*. For, as the prophet says "*The Lord is good to all, And His mercies are over all His works*"(Psalms 145:9). So that by a common instinct of nature, although the divine essence is in every way honored and worthy of goodness, all mankind truly perceives God through His own goodness more than through any other of His properties. And God's goodness is manifested in such a way in the creation of all things in their existence, even in an existence so excellent that if you ask all His creatures one after another and if they were able to answer you what could have induced God to create them, they would respond unanimously it was by His goodness. This is why King David presents so often the terrestrial and celestial beings, some gifted and some deprived of intelligence, and whatever other natures they may be, all as being engaged in the celebration of this particular virtue of goodness, and he continually invites them to remain as such in celebration. Now the actions of goodness have no other motive than that of goodness itself, that is, the desire to express oneself in giving that which one does not absolutely need but which he desires, to provide evidence of the affection which one has toward Him. Because of the virtue of goodness, the being and inclination to do good to others, seeks the good itself as an object toward which to

---

[1] Or "glory is the necessary result."

exert itself, but the one who exerts it does not have the goal of his action outside of himself, that is, outside of the desire to act in accordance with his own inclination. And the greater and more refined a goodness truly is, the more it is removed from all other reasons or causes which dilute it in the production of its actions. Thus, the goodness of God being not only grand and exquisite but also infinite in proportion with His nature and having no other cause than Himself in the creation of things, in which was given to creation to be what they had not been and to each according to its constitution an existence gifted with all the perfections befitting its species, it does not seem that one ought to complicate anything or think that God has any other aim than this—His being good. It is in connection with this that His creatures are the more obligated to consecrate themselves entirely to that end which we have said ought to be natural to them, that is to know the glory of their Creator, since He has brought them into the world and gifted each with such excellent faculties and with such precious forms, and since He has supported and preserved them by such an attentive providence solely for their sake and protected only by His pure goodness, rather than imagining in themselves that He has merely created them for Himself and sought in them purely and simply His own glory. Since as in the exercise of generosity or bigheartedness, one feels more obligated to him who does good only because he loves him, than to him who as this dispenser of good deeds seeks the reputation of liberality; therefore, created beings, if they have some knowledge and some feeling of their Benefactor, show themselves more bound to the advancement and celebration of His glory, when they see shining in their own created selves His pure goodness. If it may be said that the most excellent causes purpose for themselves the best of all ends, and that of all the ends the best is the glory of God, then it is certain that for the actions of creatures there cannot be a better end than the glory of the Creator, and unquestionably there cannot even be any that equal it. For it is the seeking of His glory with all sincerity and zeal that composes the highest plane of their piety and their virtue. For this reason the Apostle exhorts us so expressly to direct all our actions and all our thoughts toward it (His glory). But with regard to the actions of God Himself, it seems that it is more fitting to Him to be good, and to act out of His own nature of goodness alone because He is good, than merely to seek the glory of being good. Even though the highest part of duty and the greatest excellence and perfection of actions of the creature comprise the obtaining of His glory Who has directed such and unspeakable goodness toward it, it does not follow, however, that the greatest excellence of the actions of the Creator consist in desiring to appear and to be recognized as good; rather, it consists in itself as the essence of pure goodness.[1]

[21] Therefore the principle end to which God sought in the creation of the universe was that He willed to reveal His own goodness both in nature and in His effects, in bringing into being those things which did not previously exist and causing them to exist in an extremely suitable and content state, to the extent that each of them was able to desire happiness within the limitations of its own nature. But the natural end of the world and that which all creatures, each according to its instinct and the faculties which were given to it, ought to pursue above and beyond all other ends is the glory of Him Who in their creation displayed infinite power, incomprehensible wisdom, and a goodness which appears in some way or other[2] to exceed them both.

---

1 Or "it consists in wanting to be good."
2 Lit. *"je ne sçay comment surpasser"* or "I don't know how to surpass."

Chapter 3

Why God Created Man in Particular

[22] If it was the goodness of God which properly prompted Him to create all things, as we have just briefly deduced, and if the measure of His goodness may be recognized through the effects which proceed from it, man having greatly received in his own creation incomparably more favors[1] than any of the other things which we see in all of the universe, it can be stated in greater terms of man than of the other creatures, that it was a singular goodness which created him and to which therefore he is indebted in a singular way. Since for some of His creatures God gave only their existence; to others He gave life in addition to mere existence; to others in addition to existence and life, He gave sensation; but to none of these visible and corporeal things did He give the intelligence which He gave to man. So then, having existence in common with all things and life in common with the plants and sensation with the other animals, man also has the particular prerogative of having a reasonable soul which is able to contemplate the works of God and a corporeal form very wonderfully composed to devote itself to true contemplation and to make good use of it in recognizing his Creator and the particular duties by which he is called to serve His glory. Thus the Apostle says, *"what may be known about God is plain to them, because God has made it plain to them. For since the creation of the world God's invisible qualities—his eternal power and divine nature—have been clearly seen, being understood from what has been made, so that men are without excuse"* (Romans 1:19–20). And it follows for His goodness and for His wisdom together, that God was not content to give to man an understanding,[2] that is a faculty by

---

1   *Graces,* such as beauty or reckoning with God, a relationship with the Creator.

2   It appears that Amyraut is referring here to an already completed understanding and self-perception of man's own nature along with God's existence and nature as prefixed in mankind's mind. Thus, man would be created by God to seek for God as the referent of his own soul and

which man is able to devote himself to these things by itself. For God indeed established this faculty in such integrity that as soon as man began to use his intelligence, and he began to act upon it as soon as he was created, he acted in that very integrity and drew from his intelligence fruits which conform as much to the beauty and perfection of its object, who is God Himself manifested in His works which present themselves before his eyes, as to the integrity of the faculty which was the understanding itself created with a marvelously beautiful and perfect constitution.

[24] Now, this is principally that which constitutes the excellence of man, and the most precious testimony of the goodness of God toward him. Since man is naturally composed of his understanding, which governs him and holds dominion[1] over his soul and the reins of all his emotions,[2] his understanding can only have been so complete and so radiant from this recognition of its Author that man's will is kindled afresh from His love and from all His fitting and tender emotions[3] to whatever can serve His glory.[4] And since it is in this excellence that man displayed the sanctity and the goodness of his Creator, this is also the particular reason why it is said of him that he has been *"created in His image"* (Genesis 1:26). For all the creatures of God truly bear an infinity of testimonies of the virtues which He has exercised in their creation, and especially of that one virtue which He loves beyond the others, namely His goodness. But other creatures have not been made participants in them so as to possess similar virtues themselves, not having the faculty of intelligence which is absolutely necessary to the others. However, God not only displayed these virtues in the creation of man, but in this excellent faculty, He had given to him that which makes him man, specifically a ray of His intelligence, and in this like manner, the ruling principle of the virtues which represent His own.

[25] Nevertheless, the goodness of God did not stop there in its own place, but had desired that His image shine in man completely. For in God there are two things which are completely inseparable one from another: (1)

---

existence and by doing so, man would be employing his God-given ability to reason through intelligence and experience in the process of seeking after God.

1   *Tient l'empire de son ame.*
2   *Affections.*
3   *ne fust embrasee de son amour, et toutes ses affections duites et soupples …*
4   Throughout the treatise, Amyraut refers to a tri-partite constitution of man. His trichotomous description of man is as follows: man's understanding (reason) controls his emotions (desire), which are ultimately displayed in action through man's will (his choice or movement).

the first is that God is extremely good and holy; (2) the second is that God is extremely content and remains in a condition in which He lacks nothing for his happiness and glory. Thus, divine "qualities" exist, if one wants to use this term, which must correspond in constituting the condition worthy of that which is signified by the glorious name of Divinity. Although the first might be much better, more excellent, and more esteemed than the second, they are so closely linked that without the second it seems that there is something defective in the first. Thus, if not in His nature itself and, as one speaks, in His essence, these qualities exist in His necessary and dependent attributes which follow. Therefore, so that one might observe in man the whole image of God, not only in respect to the first of these things but also with regard to the second, God wished to add to the perfection of wisdom and virtue a condition in every way fortunate and glorious. And this God accomplished by placing man in a pleasant home[1] beyond our present comprehension and giving him the lordship over all His creatures. The Prophet of God undoubtedly speaks to this stating, "*When I regard your heavens the work of your fingers, the moon and the stars that you have arranged, I say, 'What is mortal man that you should remember him, and the son of man that you should visit him.' For you made him a little lower than the angels, and crowned him with glory and honor. You have given him dominion over the works of your hands, you have set all things under his feet*" (Psalms 8:3–6).

[27]   In fact, the wisdom of God and particularly His goodness required that He unite in this manner these two things. For apart from the fact that it is not appropriate that one so blessed with this first kind of perfection (goodness) should endure evil in that which concerns the other (contentment), good and evil whatever else they are, are such that they are not suitably joined together. Then, how is it that the One who had demonstrated so great a goodness towards all His other creatures, would have wished to allow the failure concerning this one,[2] in this thing which concerns so much the well being of man's existence? Indeed, how is it that the One who had caused man to be conscious of Himself by giving him this perfection in holiness and virtue, a goodness which surpasses by far that which His other creatures had experienced, should have so failed in that which was absolutely necessary to

---

1   *une demeure delicieuse* ....

2   *eust voulu permettre qu'elle eust esté si defaillante alendroit de celle-cy* ... Amyraut here speaks of the sin of Adam and the subsequent fall of mankind (Romans 5:12) which indubitably destroyed both man's goodness and his contentment, both which were to reflect the Lord's image above every other creature God ordained.

render God's image complete in him in every respect? But as it is impossible in view of this goodness that man could have been holy and virtuous and nevertheless also destitute of things that are necessary for his happiness,[1] so it is impossible that he is able to retain the enjoyment of this happiness having fallen from God's holiness. For as the image of God cannot be perfectly fulfilled by the possession of piety and virtue alone, if it is accompanied by calamity and misery—since in God these two things, holiness and contentment, are inseparable—so also this part of God's image which consists in happiness is not able to survive in the creature apart from participation and continuation in the other which lies in the perfection of God's holiness and virtue. And as neither the wisdom nor the goodness of God can permit the perfectly holy and virtuous creature to be so miserable by joining, contrary to their natures, virtue with calamity, so also neither His wisdom nor His justice can allow the creature (fallen from his integrity and having become evil), to be so content by joining happiness with vice[2] contrary to all reason.

[29]   In summary therefore, it is sufficiently clear that the reason why God created man was that God was not satisfied with the measure of goodness which He had exercised toward His other creatures, but wished to surpass Himself in displaying incomparably more in the creation of man by giving this degree of perfection and contentment which constitutes His image, to which the others could not attain. And consequently it is clear that the end[3] for which He had destined man in creating him was to establish His image in him composed of and completed by both these parts: (1) a perfection of holiness and of virtue from which he lacks nothing and (2) a contented condition in every way the same. And this He accomplished so that the one depends upon the other. If man (Adam) had stood firm in his integrity, his happiness would have also in the same way been permanent. Having fallen away from the holiness in which he had been created, man ought to lose his happiness and fall into a misery proportionate to the magnitude of the sin of the creature which rebels against his Creator and of a finite nature which violates the majesty of an infinitely glorious essence.[4]

---

1   *Beatitude*, happiness or blessedness.
2   Sin or evil.
3   *La Fin* ... the end goal or objective of one's life.
4   Amyraut throughout holds to a firm state of man's depravity based in mankind's federal union with the first man, Adam. In the following chapters, Amyraut will develop his understanding of the

CHAPTER 4[1]

WHY GOD PERMITTED THE FIRST MAN TO SIN

[32]   Now it is clear, not only by the Word of God but by common experience also, that man who had been created as such has fallen from this contented and perfect state and this has occurred through man's own fault, and consequently, man has distorted the design of his creation. For, having been destined to bear the image of God in virtue and in happiness, by permitting his integrity to be corrupted through the temptation of Satan, man allowed himself to fall from good fortune, so that God had placed him into an extremely miserable condition. And in this reality of the fall, there is no difficulty in demonstration, for it is self-evident that it has happened.[2] The complete difficulty consists in knowing why God, having been so good to man as to position him in such a high degree of perfection and happiness, has permitted him to fall and has allowed him to be overtaken by the temptation of evil. For why should God have demonstrated such a great goodness if it was to be eventually useless? And if God was able to prevent such a great misfortune, why didn't He so command before it happened so as to sustain man in the enjoyment of the blessedness that He had granted him, considering that it was principally a question of conserving the holiness and virtue of man in which consist this excellent image of the Creator and which He loves far beyond all other things? And if God was not able, how could He be all-powerful? More over, why

---

doctrine of Hamartiology (sin), demonstrating man's spiritual inability to seek or receive salvation within his own person outside of the regenerative grace of the Trinity.
   1   In Amyraut's original edition (1634), chapter four is mistakenly labeled as chapter three. Perhaps Amyraut's rush to print was the cause of this oversight.
   2   *Car qu'il en soit arrivé ainsi, la chose parle d'elle mesme...* "since this has thus happened, the thing (reality) speaks for itself."

did God give either the devil or man in their creation some faculty which not only would be able to resist God's will but could be able to reject[1] it?

[32] To say that God gave to man a certain freedom of will upon which his actions so depend from the beginning that God was not able to hinder it without doing some sort of violence to him and not able to strip him of it without removing inseparable conditions from his nature which God has graciously given to him in creation, is to limit strictly the power of God and conversely to extend even further (unnatural) human powers to man. Yet, how so? Would God, who by His providence governs all other things which He has created by His goodness and power, so limit Himself that He would exclude from His guidance the most excellent of His creatures so that man himself becomes entirely and absolutely the master of his own actions and does so whereby he does not depend in any way upon God's counsel? Or will God's wisdom have so failed in our creation that while, in forming all the other creatures—He knew how to give them faculties that He is able to rule and govern so as to accomplish in the world all that pleases Him without in any way constraining them or stripping them of the conditions and inclinations which He has given to them—He was not able to give the same to man for whom He reserves such dominion? But why? It manifestly appears that the fact that he has fallen from his fortunate state ought to be attributed to this, that there were alleged to him reasons which made him believe that in disobeying his God he could do a thing useful and advantageous for himself. For the devil showed him that the fruit was pleasant to look at and good to eat, and he persuaded him that it was able to fill him with knowledge equal to that of God himself (Genesis 3:6).[2] And this is why the Apostle says expressly that Eve *"was deceived"* (2 Corinthians 11:3). So that it is necessary to attribute this sin to a vicious error of his understanding before giving any blame or assigning the cause to man's will, which desired the things that the understanding had presented to it as desirable.[3] Could

---

1 *Vaincre.* Lit. "conquer" it. Amyraut is setting up the implausibility of libertarian free will.

2 Genesis 3:6 states, "*When the woman saw that the fruit of the tree was good for food and pleasing to the eye, and also desirable for gaining wisdom, she took some and ate it. She also gave some to her husband, who was with her, and he ate it.*"

3 Amyraut here uniquely distinguishes between man's mental capacity and his subservient will. For Amyraut, the will enacts what both the mind (the center of understanding and reason) along with the emotions (the seat of desire) dictate. Later, Amyraut distinguishes that within man's depravity his desire (emotion) is morally corrupt and incapable of desiring good or godliness on its

not God therefore, without having in any way violated his understanding, have made him realize the vanity and the falsity of these reasons so that he might have rather remained true to the God of truth than allowed himself to be moved by the persuasions of the "father of lies?"[1] Certainly this could have easily been accomplished by illuminating man's understanding to the recognition of the truth and helping him perceive the pernicious lie[2] and the poison that the devil hid under these appearances. And such that it is, illumination was so far from destroying the nature of man's understanding that, on the contrary, it is in this powerful knowledge which His excellence consists.

[35] But given that there is in man a certain freedom of will it still would have been, it seems, more expedient for him that God had removed it from him, rather than to allow him to use it in the face of the inevitable peril of such a dreadful ruin. For when, whether by the error of the understanding or by the perversity of the will, a man throws himself over the edge of a precipice in order to get bruised upon the points of the rocks we put a hand on his collar and stop him in spite of himself, far from this violence being a wrong done to him so that he should have a subject for complaint; he is, on the contrary, obliged to us for his life. Consequently, if this were the only consideration, we would have rather complained to ourselves in similar fashion either because God would have given us this freedom of will or because in our need He would not have removed it from us. Thus, the difficulty still remains, and whatever opinion one holds in these seemingly difficult and half inexplicable theological questions, it is important in any case either to resolve them or to suppress and pass over them modestly in silence. But since it can be said that God has permitted the fall, and since we find ourselves almost equally prevented from explaining it, and since the discussion of a thing so profound serves so little in the deciding of our controversies, is it prudent or modest to attempt to resolve it or is it more loving to draw out the matter, disputing the views one against the other?

[36] Truly at this point modesty is very much recommended to us, since it seems that the Holy Spirit expressly joins our modesty through His own

---

own, but that mind and reason can still function, though the mind or mental assent is insufficient in itself to form saving faith. The terminology here used by Amyraut, though, may still be interpreted as incongruous with the traditional Reformed understanding of man's constitution post-lapse.

1 John 8:44.
2 *La fraude pernicieuse* ... or "causing him to perceive the pernicious deceit."

silence. For ordinarily when Scripture makes mention of some great and notable sin which is underscored[1] and accentuates important consequences, Scripture speaks of the operation of the providence of God and expressly wants it to be duly noticed: for example, by Judas betraying our Lord or by the Jews crucifying Jesus, these did nothing except what the hand and the counsel of God as beforehand determined ought to be done;[2] further, Joseph did not go down into Egypt only by the treachery and inhumanity of his brothers, but rather by the will of God;[3] the children of Eli did not respond to the rebuke of their father because the Lord wished them to die;[4] David, cursed by Shimei, said that it was God Himself who commanded him to curse him;[5] Absalom committed his infamous sins in broad daylight because the Lord had determined it so;[6] Pharaoh did not obey the commands of God because God had hardened his heart and wanted to demonstrate His own power through him;[7] and so also of others throughout Scripture. However, here where it is a question of the first of all sins which consequently resulted in all others, the original sin which opened the door for death to envelop the whole human race and ruin the world from top to bottom, neither does history recount to us nor do all the books of the Old and New Testaments which have come since in any way speak of the intervention of the providence of God in the administration of the things which occur here. It is as if the Holy Spirit had expressly wanted to pull the curtain over this matter and teach us that in it there are abysses which are impossible to sound.

[38] And nevertheless such is the correspondence that the parties within the Christian Religion have with one another that, even if it is not possible to gather enough light to dissipate[8] all the darkness of this mystery and to lead us to its bottom depth, we can at least find enough, if we exercise a little modesty, to remove the scandal that the carnal reason of man encounters here.[9] For I ask you, as much as we have praised the goodness of God (and we

---

1 *Tiré apres soy des suites importantes* ... lit. "pulled out or plucked out."
2 Acts 4:27–28.
3 Genesis 45:7–8.
4 *L'Eternel.* 1 Samuel 2:25.
5 2 Samuel 16:10.
6 2 Samuel 12:11–12.
7 Exodus 9:12–16.
8 *Esclairer* ... more accurately "to lighten."
9 Here Amyraut ensconces one of his purposes within the treatise which is to quell the debate

could never praise it as it deserves, even if we were completely overwhelmed[1] in praise), has that in any way taken from Him the freedom to use it as it pleases Him and to bestow according His will the measure of His graces? He is God indeed, in that He is good. But He is also God in that He is elevated infinitely above all His creatures and is not obligated to anyone for anything. Had God left man in the nothingness from which he was created and left him in a condition very inferior to the one in which God had placed him, could He have been subjected to complaint in that? So far from being subjected to any complaint was He that, if immediately after having created mankind He had plunged them in hell without consideration for any of their actions either good or bad, and if He had judged it expedient to so demonstrate His sovereign imperative which He has over all things whatsoever, the creature's (mankind's) part would be to acquiesce, being nothing except what the Creator has made him to be; being God, it is to Him alone an absolute right to ordain as it seems good to Him. Would the fact that He has shown man such goodness, and if the only purpose He had in creating man was to make him feel God's own goodness, would He have diminished His right over us so as to obligate God to do more good to us? Or should the reality of God's sovereignty have increased our audacity to call into question or even to attribute as criminal His providence? For certainly, no matter how badly man may abuse His graces, they are graces nevertheless. No matter how little use the goodness of God may have been to him because of the inconsistency of his spirit, it doesn't mean that it was not still marvelous in its place.[2] It would be an excessively perverted judgment to measure God's goodness by the ingratitude of man, rather than by the goodness in itself.

[40] Concerning the accusation that the love that God carries for the piety and virtue in man as in His own image should have prevented sin from being committed, is preposterously to complain that God endured sin against Him only once in the beginning, though He has since suffered everyday in many thousands of places in the world. For piety and holiness were not more beautiful nor more lovable at that time than they are now, and nevertheless, He permits them to be violated daily. And sin is not less

---

concerning the nature of God's goodness and charity within predestination as it is misunderstood between "the parties of the Christian Religion," be they Reformed or Roman Catholic.

1 *Fondus* ... melted or sank as being "overwhelmed" in worship.
2 *Elle ne laisse pas d'avoir esté merveilleuse en son endroit.*

horrible and detestable[1] now than it was at that time and, nevertheless, He permits it to be committed continually. Thus, one should either complain in much stronger terms with the overtly profane about God's present providential rule or he should challenge with exasperating defamations[2] with the overtly profane the very first act of God's providence in actually allowing sin to occur. How so? Certainly, in that God is in Himself so holy and does nothing which would not exactly conform to the eternal rules of justice, in that He has created man in a perfect integrity and has given him inviolable laws, in that He punishes those in such a terrible manner who break them, and in this principally, as we will see below, that He has procured the redemption of man and the restoration of the world in such an amazing manner so as to destroy the works of sin and also restore the praiseworthy image of His holiness both in man and in the world; thus, He has demonstrated clearly enough what love He has for the one and the hatred He has for the rest of these things. And, therefore, this consideration has not required Him to bind His hands nor to impose His laws, in order to enlarge or to restrict or do anything against His will toward the measure of His gifts to men.

[41] There is more. The goodness of God is a great verity; but in addition, He is able to dispense His goodness with a sovereign freedom. More so, it appears still, even in this occasion, that He does so with wisdom. Man having been created in a state of perfection, nevertheless, the degree of this perfection did not exceed the measure of a natural condition which is accompanied by disadvantage.[3] For man's body was exquisitely composed, but partook of nothing beyond nature, however, and the life that he lived was an animal within nature. He ate and drank and slept and was subject to all other things of like kind. And for this reason it is said and diligently observed by the Apostle, in contrasting his condition with that which surpasses nature, *"that he has been made a living soul"* (Genesis 2:7) and he calls this condition, *"flesh and the blood"* (1 Corinthians 15:45), as an expression used in the New Testament to designate the state of nature with its accompanying, necessary weaknesses.

The faculties of man's soul which made him man were excellent in themselves and suitably arranged; nevertheless, their constitution was only natural and the holiness which resided therein proceeded from their natural

---

1 *À haïr* ... "hated or despicable."
2 *Importunes calomnies* ... "persistent slanders."
3 *Infirmité* ... "weakness or handicap."

constitution and not from any other principle. For example, just as the eye, which is naturally well composed, judges objects for itself without having further need of any supernatural assistance, so the understanding, which is the eye of the soul, was constituted, if I can use the term, in a manner so exquisite having come so recently from the hand of such a perfect Workman, and received also the objects which were offered to it without need of grace which surpassed the measure of nature. The happiness which man possessed again was natural and also the covenant by virtue of which he possessed it was also natural. For it remained solely within the communion between the Creator while it dwelled in him entirely, and was founded in the love that the worker had for his work when he saw in it the perfection that God had put there before it had become corrupted and remained no longer whole.[1] But to whatever point of perfection nature was perfected, it still had the deficiency of being changeable. And this condition accompanied it so necessarily and inseparably that, without it, it would have been nature in name only. Thus, this state of perfection was, by nature, subject to change. Yet, how can it be surprising if something that is subject to the process of maturation, actually does change? If, therefore, God had created man so that it was impossible for him to sin, He would not have placed him in the state of nature, but rather in a supernatural condition. But what exists in the natural state or animal state of being should exist first, according to the Apostle, and that which is spiritual and supernatural comes after.[2] And to raise man from the state of non-existence out of which he was drawn to an existence and then to a supernatural state, without allowing him to experience the environment of the natural condition, would not have been suitable to this intelligence which conducts all things with such marvelous wisdom.[3] It was necessary, therefore, that the first man, created from the earth, have earthly

---

1 *Rien d'avantage*. It is unclear if Amyraut is qualifying the happiness or the state of the covenant in this sentence, as his description could refer to either or both simultaneously. Either way, Amyraut makes clear that whatever man possessed before the fall was God-given, God-purposed, and "natural" as existing within the right state between God and man in which man functions using all his God-granted abilities (*faculties*). Amyraut's point is that man's subsequent fall changed that reality concisely on the earth.

2 Cf. 1 Corinthians 15:42–54.

3 Amyraut is not here declaring a rationalistic deduction that God is limited in His actions toward man, but rather inductively explaining what he sees taking place biblically in the process of God's creation of man, man's initial perfect constitution, the subsequent fall, and how the consequences of the fall have interacted with man's nature until he is redeemed and ultimately glorified.

(natural) qualities suitable to his origin—an origin that is corruptible and mutable as all the things which are made of the material elements—before the second Adam descended from the heavens, to Whom alone, as to a supernatural and heavenly principle, it belongs to communicate to those who have communion with His heavenly and incorruptible qualities.[1] Yet, what if God had not wanted to place man in an entirely supernatural and immutable state but wanted rather to supply him occasionally with the power necessary to prevent what could have happened, that is his mutation[2] from happening, and thus render him impenetrable to the strokes of evil? This would always have been a grace given above nature, which exceeded the measure of the covenant between God and the creature and the measure of the love on which it was founded. For the power of this covenant depended upon the happiness of man which would itself last only as long as his own holiness remained constant, and the love upon which it depended was of itself limited by the constancy of the integrity of the creature. Therefore, the will to render this integrity permanent and immutable would have risen a degree beyond and belonged to some other kind of goodness and to some other sort[3] of covenant.

[45] Finally, mankind is far from having a just subject of complaint against the providence of God in this action, in which man was not only able to use so much freedom but in which he even has discovered so much wisdom, we have every reason to admire in it the thoughts of mercy which He has shown in this occasion. That is that, being completely free, if God had so desired not only to let man fall as He did, but also to allow man to remain eternally in his ruin. Instead it has pleased Him to use the occasion of man's fall to redeem[4] him in an entirely commendable manner so as to make His goodness exceed the bounds of nature and to overwhelm the whole world with His mercy. How? By sending His only Son into the world to die ignominiously not only to repair the image of God which had been effaced by sin within man, but also to lead man to a point infinitely surpassing the measure of nature by virtue of a supernatural covenant.[5] For this covenant has for a Reconciler and

---

1   1 Corinthians 15:47–55.
2   i.e. the fall.
3   *Espece* … "species or kind."
4   *Relevant* … reestablish, literally "raise again," as in to restore.
5   Notably, Amyraut first implies his unique covenantal methodology here at the end of the fourth chapter. Demonstrating the historicity of Christ's atoning sacrifice as an exemplar of God

a Mediator the One who descended from heaven and who is called in this respect, in contrast to the former state as I have touched upon above, 'the Second Adam who is heavenly.' These reasons would diminish the scandal that the flesh finds in this matter or even remove it entirely, if the flesh were not so carnal, being curious, audacious, and profane.

"overwhelming the world with His mercy," Amyraut here declares that the biblical covenant of grace accentuates Christ's work as both Reconciler and Mediator between holy God and sinful man. Amyraut contends that within a universal atonement and a universal offer of redemption toward all mankind, Christ's perfect atonement procures for (faithful) mankind a true restoration of God's image within and an opportunity to be transformed into the supernatural (glorified) state whereby Christ's righteousness imputed to man allows him to stand rightly before holy God in worship and adoration forever. Amyraut states that *the* pivotal event in biblical history, where this transformative reality occurred for all the world, conditionally materialized in the covenant of grace which unfolded on the cross. Hence, covenantalism will become Amyraut's principle method later to define and explain the mystery of predestination.

CHAPTER 5

WHAT ARE THE CONSEQUENCES OF THE FIRST MAN'S SIN

[47] Man could not fall from the state in which his Creator had placed him, without two consequences necessarily following: the first being that man could not lift himself up again and the second being that he actually involved his entire race in this condemnation. In regard to the first, the state in which he had been placed consisted, as I have said, in two things, a perfect contentment and an incomparable holiness. Having once lost this integrity, how could man have been able to recover it by himself? For two motives alone are able to induce us reasonably to holiness. The first is the actual love of holiness itself as a thing marvelously beautiful, honored, and lovable, and representing the image of the One who is supremely good. The second is the love which we have for ourselves, which causes us either to desire and hope for the reward which God in His goodness has attached to virtue or to fear the punishment which follows sinfulness according to the order of His justice. But as for the love of holiness, to the extent that it can arise only from knowledge of its natural excellence, there could be no place for it in man since his fall. For as the first sin of man began through the darkening of his understanding, deceived, as we have seen above, by the fallacious appearances of reason that the serpent presented to him, also the first effect of sin is to lay such a thick darkness upon the understanding that thereafter it cannot be removed except by a supernatural light.[1] And truly the integrity

---

[1] Here Amyraut clarifies that mankind's depravity reaches to the very center of man's reason and "natural" understanding, the seat of intelligence. Thus, the reality of this spiritual darkness which imbues the mind, according to Amyraut, and renders all spiritual reason as tainted or obstructed especially in matters of spiritual adjudication—though man can still exercise the natural function of reason with a dark bent—can only be supernaturally removed by God's Spirit.

of understanding consists in perfect knowledge of the good and honest things which constitute the image of the holiness which is in God and upon that integrity depends the steadfastness of the control[1] that man ought to have over the appetites of his body so as to subdue them to reason.[2] Thus, when he caused this knowledge to be lost, he also lost the restraints which had previously governed his appetites and they, being destitute of government and direction, were put in such marvelous disorder that it was impossible for anything more dignified[3] to remain in his actions. Yet, in this confusion how could the restitution of the good order come about? It would not be the appetites themselves which of their own instinct conform themselves to the moderation which would be fitting for them in the integrity of their nature. Not being rational in themselves, they only submit to the laws of reason through the dominion of that superior faculty where reason resides. The Poets say this of the *Horses of Phaeton*, which once having broken loose and begun to cross the universe, might never have returned to the harness or resumed their ancient paths in the heavens, if the Sun, which was alone able to control them, had not itself set its hand to it. Wouldn't this also be true of understanding? For understanding itself being blind does not see the way that it ought to follow and the appetites like uncontrolled horses take the bit in their the teeth, and gallop in an twisted and irregular course with all abandon, dragging understanding itself miserably backwards.

[50] More so, there is this difference between understanding becoming dark and the driver of a chariot who has lost control over his horses, that the latter ordinarily recognizes clearly their impulse and tries to remedy their violence. If they carry him away it is at least to his great regret. Thus, he does all that he can do to resist. However, the former takes pleasure in the disorder of its passions and grows accustomed to it so that instead of resisting, it favors and takes pleasure in their wildest escapades. And this is

---

1 *La fermeté de l'empire* ...lit. "dominion over his kingdom."

2 Amyraut denotes that man's reason should dictate the movement of both his desire and will, resulting in an action which reflects understanding (godly or carnal) and reflects a mind bent toward God or self. The accentuation of the mind and man's cognitive capacity pre and post-fall figure significantly in Amyraut's theology. In the following paragraphs, Amyraut poetically describes man's marred and depraved constitution after the fall; in short, Amyraut contends that man, *in toto*, is morally depraved and tripartite incapacitated, spiritually dead and lost apart from the Spirit's regeneration—upholding a Reformed orthodox perspective of total depravity.

3 *Composé* ... "composed" or controlled as in anything praiseworthy or holy.

what the Holy Scripture calls *"being a slave to sin"* (Romans 6:16–17), a phrase which it repeats often for emphasis. For as slaves are under the control of their masters and absolutely subject to their command, not being able to free themselves from their slavery, so also man is not able to deliver himself from sin. Therefore, unless some greater virtue acts on his behalf, a superior power which sets him free, corruption will reign. It is true, however, that since the dominance which masters have over their slaves is only corporal, if slaves are not able to resist in fact, they at least spurn[1] within their will, knowing that there is not just one in a thousand who would not love to be more free. But this domination by sin is in the spirit, in the understanding, I say, in the will and in all the appetites of the soul. All of the movements of the spirit are mutually dependent in such a way that this servitude is necessarily voluntary. For since neither the understanding conceives, nor the will chooses, nor the appetites desire anything whatever against themselves, it is impossible to imagine that they would be able to be subject to any sort of constraint.[2]

[51]   As for the love that we have for ourselves and which shows itself in the fear of punishment and in the hope of reward, it does not have the capacity[3] to restore in us the integrity of our nature. Concerning our reward, how shall we be able to hope for it, if God, in whose hand it is, does not promise it to us? Now we have said above that in the state in which we were first created and at the very origin of our nature, He had joined these two things with an inseparable bond, namely the perfect integrity of the soul and accompanying (complete) happiness. Where one fails, the other is useless. The conscience then, rendering prior testimony to the man who has sinned that he is not in this integrity, ought also to plunder every hope of happiness. And far from him being able to have some such hope left in his soul, it is necessary for the same reason that he remain in continual fear of punishment. Why do I say fear? This word in our common usage seems to include some uncertainty of fulfillment, of the kind which has more the appearance that evil will more certainly come than will not. However, rightly or wrongly,

---

  1   *Regimbent* ... "to winse, kick, spurn, or strike back with the feet." See Randale Cotgrave. *A Dictionarie of the French and English Tongues*. London: Adam Islip, 1611, "REG."
  2   Here Amyraut affirms that depravity's hold on man's constitution is so complete that man's very understanding, desire, and will each now only and "naturally" superintend what is evil and are each constrained and mutually connected by their now corrupt ability to sin and remain enslaved to sin.
  3   *Efficace* ... "efficacy."

there remains some small fiber of hope and we flatter ourselves with such a pretense to avoid that which threatens us. But here that is not the case. For sin being so evident and the pronouncement of punishment irrevocable and the wrath which bears full vengeance so inflexible and relentless, the inevitable certainty of God's judgment transforms fear into despair, indeed, into an inconsolable despair. Now, as all fear of this kind is voluntarily accompanied by hate, for we naturally hate those from whom we anticipate an evil, so all despair is naturally accompanied by rage. And it should not be doubted that the despair of obtaining forgiveness—to which the devils themselves have been subject from the beginning—has only helped make them so much more evil and irreconcilable enemies of God and everything which pertains to His glory. But even if this was not the case (in spite of the truth being completely obvious and experience itself confirming it), since we have shown above that the first motive, that is the love of holiness itself, can have no place in man in view of his state of corruption, all the love that we could convey toward Him out of self interest would still not be able to repair the corruption of our nature. For who as king would love his subjects if he was persuaded that they only obey him out of fear of the gallows,[1] or as a father would love his children if they only love him in case he might disinherit them, or even as master would love his servants who follow none of his order except to the degree that they see the cross and the scourge? If, I say, while those subjects hate their prince in the depth of their hearts, if those children disdain their father, if those slaves murmur unceasingly and pronounce curses under their breath against their master, certainly the perfection of our nature does not consist in our ardent and passionate love for ourselves which includes hating God or being laid-back and languishing toward the things which concern Him. But it is rather in that loving ourselves (for it is neither possible nor reasonable to rip out from our hearts the natural affections we have) we love God incomparably more as being—because of the excellence of His nature and the demonstration of His goodness towards us—infinitely more lovable, and in that where it is necessary to distinguish between Him and us, His love and His consideration carries over without difference to the balance. So with respect to this first part of our broken condition,[2] we are not able to repair ourselves. For the other part, the consequence is evident. For we

---

1 *Gibbet*.
2 Or preceding condition, which is notably our fallen state.

would not know how to restore to ourselves our own contentedness, if not our corrected state of being so to speak, because we feel we are worthy to be re-established by our actions. But in fact, by forcing a restoration through our own effort only demonstrates plainly that we are not worthy of it.

[55]   Concerning right state of being, however, we have already seen that we are lost; seeing, that indeed by inevitable necessity we have fallen into the extreme opposite of our rightful state, having fallen into sin and that the state of sin within us is a marvelously rooted and totally incurable ulcer. And in all actuality, it would be a ridiculous attempt to wrestle against God and extort from him by violence the things which we desire most. This would be truly daring like that of the giants of whom the poets spoke, who were immodest, and truly unbridled, but engulfed by a thunderbolt. But it was not to be necessary for lightning to chase the first man from Paradise where he had been placed, the voice of God alone being sufficient.[1] And it was not necessary to prevent his return; all that was necessary was the flaming sword of the Cherubim, which signified in my opinion the trepidations of the conscience, capable even by themselves of driving us away from God and preventing us from ever daring to turn our face toward either the good condition that we have lost or the abode of His glory.

[56]   As for the other necessary consequences of sin, it is not necessary by a long disputation to show they are inevitable. Had the creation of man been like that of angels and had they all been formed in the beginning directly by the hand of God and were not dependent on individuals through means of natural generation, it would not have been necessary that the fall of one or of many to drag all of the others into ruin. It would have been possible that many might have remained in their integrity and consequently in their blessed state. But the first man, being like the root from which all the others originated, and that happiness which he possessed having been communicated to him so that he might communicate it to his descendants, could not make them participants in it once he had been deprived of it himself.[2] It may be compared to the ordinary government policy of men, where crimes of high treason are punished in the persons of those who have committed them in such a way that the misery of their pain passes even to their posterity in the

---

1 Genesis 3:23–24.
2 Romans 5:12.

ruin of houses, the exacting of fines,[1] the defamation of their reputation,[2] and similar things. So without other consideration, the penalty of the first man, because of his sin, should have extended even to his descendants, as they experience the many miseries which followed it. And, truly, how could man not have a similarly close communion with the rest of the universe as he ought to have had with his posterity, since God had established him as its master and that it seems it was the magnificent palace, so richly furnished with all commodities, in which He had wished to place him in happiness and glory?[3] Man has therefore also fully tasted a part of God's curse against sin, and has been subject to futility because of the offense of man.[4] But the foremost and greatest evil is not the participation in the punishment, but the communication of the sin which merits it. For as leprous fathers breed leprous infants like themselves and as it is only according to the order of nature that each kind propagates after his likeness, so also a man cannot be a sinner and avoid passing this dreadful leprosy of sin to his own race. In view of this transmission of the fleshly appetites along with the substance of flesh itself to his children, and a father being only able to transmit to them such as he has, corrupted and marvelously disordered, the reasonable soul which originates otherwise is absorbed with their corruption and enslaved under their dominance, and thus will have no dominance before it has any knowledge of the dominion which it ought to exercise over them and that it was able to create order with all efficiency. It is as if in a house full of drunken and degenerate[5] servants who are audacious, insolent, and impudent, a master of a more generous propensity[6] toward truth, but nevertheless nourished and performed his duties in the midst of their debauchery, was himself accustomed to their manners since the cradle and henceforth led by his own will a life as degenerate as theirs. In such a case there would be no difference between their behavior except that his corruption is so much more horrible and damnable in that he is of an ancestry which requires generosity (nobility) and that, instead of reprimanding the evil of his servants, he sanctions them by his example and serves them by poor instruction. And this is why David

---

1 *Charges* ... "fines or duties."
2 *La fletrisseure de la renommé* ... lit. "the decaying or withering of one's renown."
3 Genesis 3:17.
4 Romans 8:20.
5 *Debauchez*.
6 i.e. noble.

says of himself that *"his mother conceived him in sin, and brought him forth in iniquity"*(Psalms 51:7); and Moses states, *"that every inclination of the thoughts of his heart is only evil continually, even from his youth"* (Genesis 6:5, 8); and Job states, *"that it is impossible to draw out anything pure from that which is impure and filthy"* (Job 14:4); and finally St. Paul remarks, *"that by nature we are all children of wrath, dead in our trespasses and sins"* (Ephesians 2:1, 3). And experience also shows this: for since not only *"by sin death has entered the world"* (Romans 5:12), but moreover that this is *its wage* and *its payment* (Romans 6:23), and that children die, even from the womb, exposing for certain that there is no greater disorder in the nature of things than little children having died even before they have seen the light of the sun. Thus, that there has occurred such disorder and corruption in their nature even from the womb is aptly called the original contamination[1] of sin. From this natural corruption, therefore, as from an inexhaustible source, comes an infinity of sins augmenting and fortifying the habits of evil by repetition, it is both inevitable that they fall into the same ruin as their father and as impossible for them as it was for him to raise themselves up again. And this is the same thing that Saint Paul affirms in those words which cannot be taken seriously enough, that *"by one man sin entered the world and by sin, death, so that death came upon all men, in as much as all have sinned"* (Romans 5:12). This death envelops all men not only in the same condemnation, but also in the same cause of their condemnation, that is, their corruption and active choice of sin.[2]

---

1 Contagion.
2 *Vice.*

Chapter 6

What Is God's Design in Sending His Son into the World

[61]   The nature of God is so perfect and His wisdom so marvelous that in all things which His creatures watch come to pass each in his own time, He has foreseen from all eternity. Also because He has foreseen that which would come to pass, since He has himself ordained it, nothing happens in the universe except by the disposition of His eternal ordination. This follows from what we have cited above for Saint Paul, namely that God accomplishes all things with efficacy according to the counsel of His will. And by this ordination He has resolved to bring to pass all those things which can be called good whatsoever they are, as well, He has also resolved to permit in a similar manner evil things, the occurrence of which is beyond all doubt; thus, the operation of His providence shows itself to be truly efficacious in the dispensing of all that is necessary for their production, since everything depends on His hand. Having therefore eternally decreed in His counsel to create man in the manner which we have described above—in a condition as perfect and excellent as the state of nature would permit, yet, nevertheless natural and mutable—He foresaw in His wisdom all things present before His eyes that the devil, envious of the prosperity of man, would try to undermine him through various temptations. Primarily, God had given man the faculties of his understanding and his will and knew of what composition[1] they were and to just what extent they would support the pressure of temptation. Secondly, since God also knew to just what extent the devil would force his temptation, and in what manner he would exercise it, and what would be the extent of his power, it was impossible for God to have avoided foreseeing this event with certainty. For knowing that the efficacy of the temptation

---

1   *Trempe.*

would most assuredly exceed the measure of resistance and having for the reasons given above and for others of which we are still ignorant, God resolved not to prevent it; how, then, could He have been mistaken concerning the outcome?[1]

[63] Experience helps a commander to judge how much he must fire a cannon to breech a tower and an engineer how many barrels of powder to blow up a rampart, even though they neither built the fortifications, nor created the ramparts, nor gave the hardness to the bullets or the potency[2] to the powder. Was God therefore unable to judge either the strength of the spirit of man to resist the temptation or the efficacy of the reasons of the temptation over the spirit of man? What if the speculation of men deceives them at times because they do not penetrate far enough into the nature of things or in their inner workings, or perhaps because there is a superior cause, namely providence, upon which all events and all power of secondary causes depend, which very often operate not only contrary to the intention of men but even beyond all their speculative knowledge. Thus, man is not able to arrive by himself at the things of God, whose knowledge deepens all things without exception and overcomes man's will of which no other cause governs.[3] He therefore foresaw that man would stumble through sin and that he would drag his whole race after him into the same calamity. So that even before the world was established and man was created He had seen the sin of man and the ruin of the world and had observed all men in general and each in particular—not confusingly or haphazardly, but distinctly and carefully prescribed, and lying in this inevitable corruption of their nature—those who were in the beginning as much as those who live at present, and as much as those who will be until the consummation of all time. For the first ages of the world are not nearer to His eyes than the latter, since all things, as I have said, are equally and eternally present in His wisdom. Therefore as He has seen

---

1 Amyraut here attests to the complete sovereignty of God in all things, even the allowance of the existence of evil to serve a divine purpose for a temporal season upon the earth. This rhetorical question implies sarcasm and sets up his point to demonstrate the sovereign plan of God in rescuing man from himself.

2 *Le violence,* explosiveness.

3 Contrary to critics that Amyraut held views of natural theology outside the bounds of Reformed Orthodoxy, here Amyraut defines that man is incapable of salvation or even spiritual knowledge of God without God's intervention, overpowering of the will, and regeneration of the mind and heart.

all mankind perishing equally without distinction or difference in the same shipwreck in a bottomless and shoreless sea, He has had compassion in this calamity and sought some means to procure the salvation of the world. And although His justice brought Him to leave men to perish as they deserved, He nevertheless permitted Himself to be overcome by His own mercy.[1]

[65] And since the misfortune of man consisted in two things, the corruption of his nature by sin and the suffering of the misery that sin naturally brought about, God could only be touched by His mercy to restore man if He resolved to restore him in these two ways, namely, the mending of his nature and the restoration of his happiness, thus restoring to man his image entirely. Yet for man, that part of his image which consists in holiness is much closer to his heart than the other and since it is more worthy of the excellence of man to be good and virtuous than to be happy and comfortable, God has shown more care and desire to repair man's holiness than his happiness, even though these two things are totally inseparable. This is why it is so true that Holy Scripture often speaks of the deliverance from the penalty that we have warranted, not concerning the joy of all sorts of contentments, but as those which encompass the salvation of man. For truly these things constitute a part of salvation and the representation of this part of salvation actively moves us by the love we have for ourselves to induce us more excellently toward faith and holiness. Thus Scripture nevertheless does not conceal that true salvation lies within the other deliverance, namely, the deliverance from the dominance of sin, and in the ultimate sanctification of both our bodies and our souls which consists of that principal part called salvation. Thus Scripture states, *"we are called to be saints, to be renewed in the spirit of our understanding and clothed in the new man; created according to God in justice and true holiness; to be swallowed up in the death of Christ through Baptism, so that as He has risen from the dead for the glory of the Father, we also in like manner should walk in newness of life,"* (1 Corinthians 1:2).[2] Thus, in general, we are to imitate the example of His holiness since we are predestined to be conformed to Him in glory. Scripture also states that Christ came *"to destroy the works of sin"* (1 John 3:8) since *"For what the law was powerless to do in that it was weakened by the sinful nature, God did by sending his own Son in the likeness of sinful man to be a sin offering. And so He condemned sin in sinful*

---

1 *Clemence* ... clemency.
2 Also Ephesians 4:24 and Romans 6:4.

man." (Romans 8:3) Further, the Bible teaches that *"It is because of Him that you are in Christ Jesus, who has become for us the very wisdom from God—that is, our righteousness, holiness and redemption"* (1 Corinthians 1:30). In a word, that *"the grace of God that brings salvation has appeared to all men. It teaches us to say no to ungodliness and worldly passions, and to live self-controlled, upright and godly lives in this present age, while we wait for the blessed hope, the glorious appearing of our great God and Savior, Jesus Christ, who gave Himself for us to redeem us from all wickedness and to purify for Himself a people that are his very own, eager to do what is good"* (Titus 2:11–14). And if we know how to honor these things as one should, the greatest good is reserved for us in heaven and consists in the fact that all *"shall be made like God, for we shall see Him as He is"* (1 John 3:2); that is, that by perfect knowledge of His admirable virtues, we will be transformed into His image. And there is no need to produce more examples in that the gospel presents and recommends it thus line by line.

[68] But here appears with marvelous clarity the wisdom and mercy of God: for He has in truth created us very good and happy in the beginning, yet also in a natural condition, meaning mutable. Therefore concerning the natural part of man, having come first and ultimately being corrupted, it was suitable to the wisdom of God—since He wanted to restore man by putting him in a supernatural condition—and by His mercy to deliver man from this condition of perilous change by making him immutable.[1] This is why as for the happiness proposed to us by a degree which surpasses much more than Adam ever possessed, be it in regards to the condition of the body, since after the resurrection it will be covered with incorruptible and heavenly qualities, or be it in regards to the home or the place of happiness, since we will be rejoicing in heaven, or be it in regards to the nature of blessings which we anticipate since they are in every way unimaginable as the Apostle says, *"No eye has seen, no ear has heard, no mind has conceived what God has prepared for those who love Him"* (1 Corinthians 2:9). In what way, then, does Adam's condition not compare? And as for holiness, it is inseparable from those to whom it has been communicated by virtue of this salvation, and cannot be shaken or overpowered by any temptation whatsoever.

[70] And the manner in which God has thus proceeded to restore the human race is wonderful in every respect. For in consideration of His infallible foreknowledge that man in his lost state was so miserable, God had in His

---

1   Or in a glorified state.

mercy a singular desire to draw man out of this miserable condition and to place him in one which is much better than from where he had fallen. This presents, it seems, an insurmountable obstacle on the part of God's rightful justice which unceasingly demands retribution[1] due to man's grave offense. And this is not merely a common retribution as such. For justice being a virtue of God and all the divine virtues which are in God exist perfectly to an infinite degree, it was necessary that God's justice demand a retribution in the fullest measure since Man's sin was specifically committed against an infinite majesty; in the very least, man's retribution should be exacted in the fullest measure that the creature is able to bear. The creature therefore being capable of bearing a penalty—not infinitely in regards to its grandeur since he is only a creature, that is to say that creature has its limitations and that it is not capable of infinite feeling, but only being perpetual, that is to say infinite with respect to its duration, since his soul is immortal—the justice of God, therefore, required that man should be punished eternally and only in a way which could be compatible with the restoration of our nature. Thus, it seems that between these things there is a non-passable abyss. And truly it is not possible for God both to restore man to a state of happiness while leaving him in that state of sin and vice, perpetual blessedness being a condition which is by the dispensation of God impossible to attain through the hatred of piety and of virtue. And it is impossible that He would reestablish man in a state of integrity and virtue without a previous satisfaction of His righteous justice. For the perfection of nature in piety and in virtue would be a much greater thing than the perfection of its condition in happiness and comfort. If therefore it agreed neither with the wisdom nor the justice of God to adjudicate to man the least good without the first and more necessary being satisfied,[2] it would have agreed easily with neither one of these to communicate to man the greater good without previous satisfaction.

[72] Man therefore not being able to provide his own satisfaction to God and no other creature being capable of such a great feat, God ordained to send his Son into the world and caused Him to put on our human nature for two purposes: the first is to satisfy the justice of God by the suffering of the penalties which we alone deserved, and by this, establishing our

---

1 Vengeance.
2 Atoned for or covered.

guarantee.¹ For by accepting this charge from the Father and offering Himself voluntarily, Christ became capable of taking upon Himself the crimes which He had not committed and which otherwise could not have been transferred if He had not so closely unified² Himself with us in flesh, sharing in our human nature, but also by an express commandment of God and through a voluntary submission to the adjudged punishment for the redemption of others. Therefore, since He became man, He was capable of actually suffering death and, in fact—it having been so decided by the commandment of His Father—Christ willingly submitted to death. Further, in that He was also eternally Holy God, He was able by His suffering to take the punishment for our offenses equal to their demerit, and by this means to satisfy, by His infinite worth, God's perfect justice. This obstacle removed, Christ paved the way for the mercy which justice had held in restraint, and had prevented from overflowing the banks for which it had been established.

[73] The other purpose is that, in consequence of His suffering to which He so freely and voluntarily submitted in order to obey His Father and to procure the salvation of the human race, Christ had the right and the honor Himself of accomplishing the work of their salvation and being the perfect example of it; to be, I say, the foremost example of it. For with respect to holiness, whether you reflect on Christ's holy life and ministry before or after His death, He has been and will be eternally without spot and without blemish and so perfectly represents the image of God in such an illustrious and glorious manner that one could well say *"whoever has seen Him has seen the Father"*³ and that *He is truly resplendent with His glory.*⁴ And with respect to happiness, Christ possesses it in a degree which surpasses all comprehension and intelligence. For Scripture expressly teaches that we ought to be *"made to conform to His glorious body"* (Philippians 3:21) and *"that we are predestined to be conformed to His image"* (Romans 8:29). Further, that *"as we have born the image of the first Adam who is of the earth, we must bear the image of the Second Adam Who is descended from heaven"* (1 Corinthians 15:47–49). This means we are to be fulfilled in Him; for it is by Him that the Spirit of sanctification has been sent so as to give the Spirit to those who belong to Him, binding them by this means and pulling together such a close communion that even the

---

1 Sureté.
2 Allié ... "as in associated or covenanted."
3 John 14:9.
4 Hebrews 1:3.

political and civil union between subjects and their princes, or the political and natural union between husband and wife, or the natural communion between vines and branches with their trunks, or soldiers with their captain are not any more firm or indissoluble. For all these comparisons are employed in Scripture to signify this communion with us and still none are adequate to explain it. Since the principle of our sanctification rests in Him as its source and since we participate in it as streams which flow from it, we ourselves are able to glory in it since we live in union with His life, that is if we have truly entered into His Body and take part in this truly fortunate communion. And it is also in Him that the same power of the Spirit resides by which He resurrected us from the dead and will clothe us with incorruptible qualities like that which He Himself possesses. Accordingly the Apostle says, *"That if the Spirit of Him who raised Jesus Christ from the dead is in us, He who raised Jesus Christ from the dead will give life to our mortal bodies also, for the sake of Him who by means of His spirit lives in us"* (Romans 8:11). And Scripture also states this very expressly in, *"that everyone who looks to the Son and believes in Him shall have eternal life, and I will raise him up at the last day"* (John 6:40). And this is the reason why it is said that *"to those who believe in Him He gives the right to become children of God"* (John 1:12) and why Scripture so often refers to our adoption in Christ.

[76] Considering, therefore, the nature of children, one customarily thinks of the following: first, they are of the same nature as their father; second, they retain this resemblance to his nature; and last, they partake in his wealth and in his inheritance, being his dependents and being, in a manner of speaking, part of his person. Thus, similarly, the restoration of holiness in us causes St. Peter to say that we *"are participants in the divine nature"* (2 Peter 1:4). And since we are participants by the efficacy of His Spirit and Word, this causes St. John to state, *"we are born of God"* (1 John 3:9).[5] That we have a part in His wealth causes St. Paul to affirm also that *"as children we are heirs of God and co-heirs with Christ"* (Romans 8:17). And that we have the feeling and the assurance of all these things in our souls by virtue of the same Spirit, makes the same Apostle say that *"He bears witness to our spirits that we are children of God"* (Romans 8:16). And nevertheless, all this is called adoption because in it the integrity of nature performs nothing, but rather the grace of the

---

5   Also 1 John 4:7.

redemption; and it is called adoption in Christ because we only have these things by His merit and His intervention.

Chapter 7

What is the Nature of the Decree by which God Has Ordained to Accomplish this Design (of Sending the Son), Both in Regard to its Extent and in Regard to the Condition on Which it Depends

[77] Since the misery of men is equal[1] and universal and since the desire that God has had of delivering mankind by such a great Redeemer proceeds from the compassion which He has for them as His creatures which have fallen into such a great ruin, and since they are equally[2] still His creatures, the grace of redemption which He has offered and procured for them ought also to be equal and universal, provided that they are also found to be equally disposed to receive it.[3] And to this extent there is no difference between them.

---

1 In Amyraut's "corrected" second edition (1658), he removed the word equal (*égale*) here since the traditionally Reformed took offense at the idea that Christ would have died universally and *equally* for all mankind's sin even if all of mankind equally are depraved and in equal need of a universal Savior. The word "equal" was more offensive initially than the word universal since some Reformed theologians could assert that Christ's death was sufficient universally in some sense, since Christ Himself is ultimately valuable and universally worthy to atone for any sin; but, few of the Reformed at this point held that Christ died equally for all *if* in fact, on the cross, He actually purchased salvation for the elect alone. For the traditionally Reformed, the equality of Christ's death as it pertains to intention or application is a non-sequitur. For an introductory statement concerning Amyraut's meaning of equality and those who repelled its use within the atonement, see Alan C. Clifford, *Amyraut Affirmed* (Norwich, UK: Charenton, 2004), 17ff.

2 (1658) edition: "indifferently" replaces "equally."

3 This sentence is the main thesis for Amyraut in this treatise or what is later called "Amyraldianism." The theory of Hypothetical Universalism derives from the Latin word *hypotheticus* or "conditional," and states that Jesus died for all universally (universal atonement), though individual salvation is based on man's (conditional) faith to trust in Christ as Savior. Thus, Hypothetical Universalism is "Conditional" Universalism in that though Jesus' death is intended universally for

The Redeemer has been taken from their race and made a participant in the same flesh and the same blood with them all, that is, from a same human nature conjoined in Him with the divine nature in a unity of person. The sacrifice that He offered for the propitiation of their offenses was equally[1] for all; and the salvation that He received from His Father to communicate to men in the sanctification of the Spirit and in the glorification of the body is ordained[2] equally for all, provided—I say—that the necessary disposition to receive it (in men) is equal in the same way.[3] It is very true that it has been promised in a particular manner to the posterity of Abraham with whom God has contracted covenants that He does not have with the other men of the world. But what there was in special regard for this nation goes back to the prophecy given from the beginning, namely that the seed of the woman would *bruise the head of the serpent*.[4] Since this truth unfortunately has remained buried in oblivion among all the rest of the posterity of Adam in all other nations, therefore God sought to renew the memory of this prophecy

---

all mankind, salvation is still conditionally based on man's faith response to Jesus as Savior. More so, Amyraut remains firmly within the Reformed theological camp since he maintains that only the Holy Spirit can regenerate man's heart toward salvation and that man's redemption is centered in God's will and work—not man's.

1 (1658) edition: "equally" removed.
2 *Destiné* ... "ordained or appointed."
3 Amyraut distinguishes himself theologically through this reasoning. Rejecting the Traditional Reformed Supralapsarian formula that (1) God decreed in eternity past to save (elect) certain individuals, then (2) decreeing to create the world, (3) allowing man's fall, and then (4) providing salvation through the cross to those elect—Amyraut maintained that God decrees (1) the creation of the world and (2) the salvation of all through Christ, but a salvation conditioned upon man's believing in or having saving faith to actually receive that salvation procured for them individually. Yet, because man cannot choose Christ naturally or be regenerated to salvation in his own power since man is utterly depraved, (3) God decrees to send His Holy spirit to regenerate the elect. The uniqueness of Amyraut's theology is that it emphasizes God's ineffable mercy and kindness toward lost man and the reality that Jesus died for all and genuinely desires the salvation of all. This theological bent is a stark contrast to the Reformed theologians and spiritual tone within Amyraut's day. Amyraut writes this *Brief Treatise* to counter the seeming harsh theological tenure of misconstrued predestination within the Reformed Church and to soften the debates both within the Reformed Church and among the confused multitudes within Roman Catholicism depicting God as a cruel tyrant who forces predestination on the unwilling and damns even the willing if they are not "elect" in eternity past. Thus, Amyraut here wants to set a new spiritual tone of hope, of God's rich mercy toward all the lost, God's provision to save all universally if they will choose Christ, and the reality that every man is responsible to receive and accept Christ as Lord and Savior.
4 Genesis 3:15.

among His people and by the means of the promises of the Redeemer Who began from that moment on within the nation of the Jews the building of His united Church; in addition this nation was to have this honor that the Redeemer would be born out of its midst, out of the seed of Abraham, its patriarch and of David the most commendable of its kings.

[79] And finally, so that the doctrine of redemption would be first preached among the Jews and by none other than the Redeemer Himself and by His Apostles, this prerogative belongs to this nation by virtue of the promises and the covenants. But in fact, all the peoples of the earth have been called to the communion of the same salvation according to the Prophets and the Apostles sent into all the world; as such they call themselves *debtors* because of the commission which had been given to them, *"as much to the Greeks as to the Barbarians, as much to the wise as to the foolish"* (Romans 1:14), concerning the knowledge of the gospel. For they have learned both from the mouth of their master and even from the revelations of the heavens themselves, that *"God does not show favoritism, but that he is attentive to those in every nation who fear him and devote themselves to doing right"* (Acts 10:34). Therefore, to the extent that the Jews have shown themselves unworthy of the special grace which has been made to them, the Apostles have felt more obligated to make the cross of Christ flourish and the doctrine of salvation to bear fruit among the other nations. Following the words of Paul and Barnabas which cannot be considered too attentively, *"it was indeed to you Jews that it was necessary to announce first the Word of God. But in that you reject it and in this judge yourselves unworthy of eternal life, behold, we turn to the Gentiles. For the Lord has so commanded us saying, 'I have ordained you to be the light to the Gentiles, so that you would bring salvation to the ends of the earth'"* (Acts 13:46–47).

[80] And truly though there are perhaps many nations to which the clear preaching of the gospel has not yet come by the mouth of the Apostles, nor of their descendants, and who do not have any distinct knowledge of the Savior of the world, it is not necessary to think however that there is either any people, nor even a single man excluded by the will of God, from the salvation that He has acquired for the human race, provided that he takes advantage of the testimonies of mercy that God has given to him. Though again He does not make known distinctly to all who this Redeemer is by whom they have been saved, such is the Providence by which He preserves them, the temporal blessings through which He arouses them and fills them continually, and the long-suffering and incredible patience which He exercises

toward them as to be sufficient preaching for them if they are attentive, in order to make them understand that there is mercy in His presence toward him, for those who respond[1] in faith and repentance.[2] Accordingly, the Apostle taught that "*the riches of His goodness and patience and of this long-suffering lead men to repentance*" (Romans 2:4). Would God, therefore, lead men to repentance for nothing, and by intention, if they came to obey the invitation and repented, to exclude them from His grace? God is too good, and, if one must use the term, too serious, to present to men vain hopes.[3] That is why it is foolish to doubt that *if* in some nation of the world where even the name of Christ is not known, if it happened that He had come across someone who, touched by the testimonies of God's mercy which He presents to all parts of men in the administration of the things within the universe, and was truly converted to Him as to obtain the salvation of

---

1 *recourent* ... "run to."

2 (1658) edition states here " ... for all those who respond in trust and repentance." The word faith (*foy*) is replaced as being too insensitive and potentially confusing since man cannot respond by salvific faith unless he is first regenerated by the Holy Spirit. The phrase as it stands may be ambiguous to that point.

3 Amyraut posits in the following paragraphs what appears to be his contention for the salvation of the heathen who have never heard of Christ. However, as will soon become clear, Amyraut is here stressing (in confusing terms to be sure) his belief that God's incredible mercy and universal desire for all mankind to be saved such that, although there is no biblical warrant or reason to believe it could be possible, that Amyraut would not be surprised if God made salvation possible through another yet undiscovered means for the heathen who had no opportunity to hear or respond to the gospel. In a sense, Amyraut is declaring that God's mercy toward the lost is unpredictable since the reality that anyone is saved at all is a testament to God's goodness and mercy and that in a realm of possibility outside of biblical knowledge, God would still be just to redeem man in any way He saw fit—though Scripture is clear that no man can be saved outside of Jesus Christ (John 14:6). However, Amyraut clearly demonstrates below that there is no salvation outside of Christ (Acts 4:12) and here accentuates that the God of salvation is a God of universal mercy and love and truly desires to save all, even *if* it were possible that men could come to faith from general revelation. The stress here is God's loving nature and infinite mercy, not man's natural capacity for salvation within nature or within himself. The next sentence underlines the very nature of God Himself as true to His own mercy, love, and desire for mankind's salvation whether one sees or not the workings of God's salvific plan on the earth among all nations.

his grace (and we will see below what faculties or power there is in man to convert himself in this way),[1] it would only give Him joy.[2]

[82] Also, even though one may not know distinctly the name of Christ and has learned nothing of the manner in which He has obtained redemption for us, he would not be left out, however, from being a participant in the remission of his sins, in the sanctification of his spirit, or in the glorious immortality.[3] For these words are eternally and universally true, that *"It is He who is the propitiation for our sins, and not only ours but also for the sins of the whole world"* (1 John 2:2). And this, moreover, that *"God desires that all men might be saved, and come to the knowledge of the truth, since there is only one God and only one mediator between God and men, that is the man Jesus Christ, who has given Himself as a ransom for all"* (1 Timothy 4:5–6). This is to say that not only does He not exclude anyone, but that it would be very easy for the entire world to draw closer to salvation, since He here invites the whole world as to a grace which He has destined for all humankind, if one does not shown himself to be unworthy. And this is why St. Paul calls it *"the grace of salvation to all men"* (Titus 2:11).

[83] And although these words, "for *God so loved the world that He gave His only Son, that whosoever believes in Him will not perish, but will have eternal life"*

---

1 Per Amyraut, actually man cannot and does not have the faculties within himself for actual salvation as stated below. Amyraut adds this parenthetical phrase to reinforce now and later in this treatise that he holds that no man can actually save himself or has enough "light" within the universe or within himself to be saved on his own or apart from Christ since man is utterly depraved and lost *until* God regenerates his heart. In chapter eight Amyraut clearly delineates man's utter depravity and inability to save himself or even rightly respond in faith apart from prior regeneration by the Holy Spirit. The point here, then, is that God has offered salvation universally through not only creation (Rom. 1:19–20), but through the testimonies of conscience, Christ's death, the gospel message, and the mysterious drawing of the Holy Spirit. Amyraut is emphatically stressing God's universal love for all heathen and the lost. Emphasis mine.

2 Again, notice the significance of Amyraut's conjectural sentence structure: he employs the subjunctive conditional phrases "if," "if it happened," and "it would," positing a hypothetical counterfactual perspective of reality which emphasizes God's universal mercy and universal offer and provision of salvation to all humanity—though not based in biblical, existential reality.

3 In this sentence too, Amyraut distinguishes to his readers that God's mercy and desire for the salvation of all men even reach as far as the far-off heathen of distance lands who have yet to hear of the gospel and that their disparate distance from the established Church or clear presentation or understanding of the gospel does not automatically discount them from being able to one day hear, respond, and find Christ's mercy in salvation in their culture or world. Amyraut's point is clear: Jesus died for all!

(John 3:16), seem to make so much this grace of God universal, as proceeding from the love that God has carried for humankind, that nevertheless it is restricted to those who *believe*, and it does not seem that those being invited to believe in Christ who have not even heard talk about Him contradicts those things which we have posited above. For as there are two sorts of preaching Christ, so also there ought to be, if an objection has not been raised elsewhere, two sorts of faith.[1] One type of preaching is by the ministry of the Apostles and of those to whom the gospel has been committed, who announce Jesus, the son of Mary, and the eternal Son of God at the same time, who redeemed us from our sins by His cross, and who being raised from the dead has ascended into the heavenly places from where we should wait for Him in our redemption. This preaching engenders a faith in the mercy of God, manifested in this great Savior and joined with a distinct knowledge of this Savior Himself, this being a faith which also produces in our spirits entirely marvelous results.

[84] The other type of preaching is by the intervention of the providence of God alone which preserves the world despite its iniquity and invites it to repentance by His great patience and, if men were not naturally blind and obstinate in their blindness, this preaching would be capable of engendering in them a faith[2] in the mercy of God; this type of preaching is deprived of the truth of the distinct knowledge of the Redeemer whom the gospel preaches, but it is sufficient nevertheless to render men joyful of salvation of which He is the author. Therefore, the ones to whom Christ is distinctively preached believe in Him through knowing Him, while the others, if they do not neglect the mercy of God that He offers to them by the leading of His providence, believe in Him without knowing Him. Now concerning that God displays in His mercy and hope within salvation to men in any manner at all, it comes from His justice that has been appeased by the sacrifice of His Son and thus, He has removed the hindrance that sin put before the grace of forgiveness, if men do not show themselves unworthy.

---

1 Traditional Reformed objections were seriously raised against the points which Amyraut here declares, and especially the confusion around the word and Amyraut's meaning of "faith." In his second edition (1658), Amyraut clarifies the word "faith" here and replaces it by "knowledge" (*connaissance*), as in "there are two sorts of knowledge" or beliefs (persuasions) in response to how God chooses to reveal the truth of the gospel—through man (apostolic evangelism) or through direct divine intervention.

2 (1658) edition: the word "persuasion" replaces the word "faith" here.

[85] Yet, all of this depends upon the principle condition that men do not show themselves unworthy. For it does not agree with the wisdom of God to procure or to propose[1] this salvation to humanity to be truly placed and in fact even with great joy to those who do not want it and who remain so stubborn as to refuse His mercy. Why do I say, it does not agree with the wisdom of God? Because it is absolutely impossible that men are saved in spite of themselves.[2] For since the principal part of salvation consists in the sanctification of the soul[3]—and this sanctification comes by the illumination of the mind,[4] the emotion,[5] and in the correction of the will so that the movements and operations of all these powers might be conformed to the will of God and represent His image in their excellence—how could all these things be activated in a man who remained nevertheless obstinately opposed to God and to all these virtues that He presents to him in His grace? As such, it is as impossible to illumine a thing which remains nevertheless darkened or to amend another which always remains bent; this would imply within itself a manifest contradiction. And since the second part of salvation could not in any way exist without the first, it was even impossible as I have said often to give man the joy of happiness without first communicating to him the sanctification of his soul. It is therefore necessary, before this Redeemer to whom has been committed the charge of accomplishing our salvation, that He display the power of His Spirit in our regeneration and glorification and make us feel the effect of His communion in these things, that men receive Him and come to be united with Him. And this is what He Himself calls, "*to come to Him, to look upon Him and to believe in Him*" (John 6:35, 40). That means to be entirely persuaded of this truth, that He is the Savior of the world, so as to seek in Him the remedy for our weaknesses. It is that which the apostles call in so many places *faith* which, if true and sincere, grafts us into the Body of our Lord Jesus as wild shoots into an ungrafted olive tree, in order to draw out of him the juice and sap of spiritual life. If it is not found in us, we remain in our corruption and natural misery.

[87] All of the New Testament teaches this to us from beginning to end. Christ, notably, does so in these beautiful passages: "*As Moses lifted up the serpent*

---

1 Offer.
2 i.e. that they continue to rebel willfully against God.
3 Or regeneration of the soul by the Holy Spirit which leads to the process of sanctification.
4 Understanding or reason.
5 Desire or affections.

in the desert, so also it is necessary that the Son of Man be lifted up, so that whoever believes in Him should not perish, but should have eternal life. For God so loved the world that He has given His only Son, that whosoever believes in Him might not perish, but have eternal life. For God has not sent His Son into the world to condemn the world, but that through Him the world will be saved. Whoever believes in Him will not be condemned, but whoever does not believe is condemned already. For he has not believed on the name of the only Son of God" (John 3:14–16). Furthermore, *"Whoever believes in me has eternal life, and whoever does not believe, the wrath of God remains on Him"* (John 3:36). And there is no need for more proofs in a thing so clear and uncontested. His beloved disciple here uses an expression with great emphasis: *"If we receive the witness of men, the witness of God is greater. For this is the witness of God, of which He has testified of His Son, that God has given us eternal life and that this life is in His Son"* (1 John 5:9–10). So that by not receiving Christ as Savior one rejects the only means of obtaining salvation, and in addition to the sin that there is in despising so great a grace which God has presented to us, there is, moreover, the crime also of accusing God of lying by not believing the testimony which He has given concerning His Son. Thus, if you consider the care that God has taken to procure the salvation of the human race by sending His Son into the world and the things that He has done and suffered to this end, God's grace is universal and presented to all men. But if you consider the condition that is inescapably appointed, which is to believe in His Son, you will find again this care of giving men a Redeemer that proceeds from a marvelous love toward the human race, nevertheless this love does not exceed the following limit, to give salvation to men *provided that they do not refuse it.* If they refuse it, He deprives them of hope and by their own unbelief they aggravate their condemnation. And in giving these words, *"God desires the salvation of all men"* (1 Timothy 2:4) this truth receives this necessary limitation, *"providing that they believe."* If they do not believe, He does not desire it. This will to make the grace of salvation universal and common to all men is in this way conditional, that without the accomplishing of the condition, it is entirely ineffectual. Let us see therefore on what the fulfilling of condition, and consequently the particular efficacy of universal grace, depends.

CHAPTER 8

SINFUL MAN'S INABILITY TO ACCOMPLISH HIS OWN SALVATION

[90] I have said above that man falling from the integrity in which he had been created, became so miserable that it was totally impossible that he could raise himself out of his own misery, and herein I had deduced sufficient reasons for the subject I was discussing. But that cannot be sufficient for the present question. For perhaps someone might say that he does not have the ability to take advantage of the Redeemer's offer by himself. However, the nature of God's justice and that of man's own sin do not permit man to be able to do so. But concerning that, does it really follow that man is not actually capable to receive a Redeemer who has procured for him salvation in the past and which God is currently presenting it to him? What great difficulty could there be in accepting the remission of his sins and the hope of life which is so freely offered to him? Certainly it does not seem at first that this ought really to be so difficult. But it is found nevertheless to be impossible in experience and Scripture testifies of this also, the reasons being manifest and pertinent. For I ask you, if there is in man some virtue which renders him capable in himself of embracing the Redeemer who is offered to him, why is it that having been preached to so many people, there are so few who believe? The Apostles have declared the doctrine to all nations and they have expounded it with marvelous clarity, while again and again they have accompanied it with the holiness of an exemplary life and works which were admirable in every respect; yet, nevertheless, they complain that there are only a few in comparison with the others, who are converted by their preaching and testimony. Since then, those to whom they gave the charge of preaching the same gospel after them propagated it with all their ability, but they found in it such a strange resistance which, not content to

merely disobey them, these persecuted them because of this doctrine to every extreme.

[92] Witness the horrible carnage that the Roman Emperors exacted from the Christians, and not only the despisal, but the abomination in which this name was held in their times among men. And if it did not happen that the populace rejected it, one would be able to accuse them of misunderstanding Christianity which played itself out negatively in many other ways. But the greatest personages over the centuries were ordinarily the most resistant: the politicians hated it; the philosophers combatted it with their subtlety and the orators with their eloquence, each vying with the other to use whatever faculty he had of the sciences in the wisdom of the flesh to oppose the course which it wished to set for the world. And concerning the obstinance of the Jews nothing else needs to be said. It was to them that the Messiah had been promised and portrayed, in a manner of speaking, in their own Scriptures. They had no other words in their mouth nor other hope in their heart than of this One who had been promised to them. The lineage from which He would arise and the place of His birth had been designated. The years ordained for His advent had expired. He presented Himself before them in the expected manner and He performed His miracles in their presence. More so, they observed[1] Him from every aspect and put Him to every test, and all the while they were not able to recognize Him. They put Him upon the cross because they were scandalized by not finding Him to their taste, and then, after having crucified Him, His cross became for them a new stumbling block.[2] After that who could doubt that there is in man a strange blindness—since the Jews plainly did not recognize Jesus as Messiah, nor His salvation, nor its Author—and consequently deprives himself of the very enjoyment of salvation?

[93] And the Scripture plainly confirms this, which reveals itself by experience. For when it speaks of the condition in which we find ourselves naturally, it gives us titles which clearly speak to this impotence: Scripture calls us *"slaves of sin"* (Romans 6:20) and as we have said above this servitude is in the soul, in the understanding, and in the will.[3] What effort then can these faculties make or what action can they produce which is not dependent

---

1 *Considerent.*
2 *Scandale.*
3 Here too Amyraut affirms that man's depravity reaches to all parts of man, his soul (the seat of emotion), his natural reason and intellect, and his will—each being enslaved to sin.

upon this principle which dominates them? Scripture states, *"the flesh is not able to be subject to the law of God"* (Romans 8:7) and teaches again and again that we are flesh. Thus, what obedience can we actually give to the One who calls us and publishes His ordinances before us? Scripture states that by nature we have *"a heart of stone"* (Ezekiel 36:26) and what ability can there be in a stone to hear the exhortations that one would give to it? Scripture also states, *"we are dead in our trespasses and sins"* (Ephesians 2:1). Now what is the possible strength of a dead man, either to raise himself up, or even to hear the voice of the One who cries to him to raise him from the tomb? And although most men reject the gospel of Christ, there are some, however, who receive Him; and when that happens, one could think that even if unbelief is common, it is not however absolutely universal, but depends upon the freedom of the will in man which expresses itself in some for good and in others for evil. Scripture, however, invariably attributes the faith by which we embrace Christ to the operation of God in us, mostly in terms which describe the utter impotence which is our part in this affair. For Scripture says that *"it is He who removes from us the heart of stone, in order to give us a heart of flesh"* (Ezekiel 36:26), and that it is He who *"transports us from the kingdom of darkness to the kingdom of light and makes in us both to will and to do His good pleasure"* (Colossians 1:13; Philippians 2:13); it is He who illumines us, who renews us, who regenerates us, who vivifies us, who makes us new creatures and creates us anew, who grafts us into the Body of His Son, who calls us, who draws us, who grants to us to believe in Christ, and similar things.[1] These words show us just how much that we contribute nothing to the efficacy by which our reason is persuaded to receive the doctrine of salvation and our wills to follow it. And so that none can doubt this, Christ himself declares this truth like a prophecy which none can oppose. He states, *"no one can come to Him"* that is, as He himself interprets, to believe in Him, *"unless the Father draws him"* (John 6:44). In light of this, who would doubt our natural impotence?

[96] In fact, if we remember the state into which we said above that we have fallen we will not be amazed by this impotence. For the doctrine of the gospel, because of the evidence of the truth, is well called a light, and Christ who is its author, the Light of the world. But if there is nothing more, it is only an external light which can only be received by a faculty which is suitably

---

1   Cf. John 3:5; Ephesians 2:5, 10; Romans 8:28; 11:23.

disposed. Our understanding, therefore, having become dark through sin and its darkness growing daily through the habit of sin—in a manner which its blindness is comparable to a cataracts which has grown over the pupil of the eye and prevents entirely the faculty of sight—is no longer able to receive this spiritual light in which the truth resides, more than any other eye which because of a film has lost the ability to see the light which the Sun lavishes upon the world. That is why the Apostle desires above all things that God would grant to men, that *"the eyes of their understanding be illumined;"* indeed, there is such great difficulty in that *"according to the surpassing greatest of His power, and the efficacy of the power of His might"* (Ephesians 1:17–18). And Christ says that it is necessary *"to be instructed by God"* (John 6:45) according to the words of the prophet, since there is no correspondence between the nature of perceiving a truth and the perverse disposition of our reason.

[97] Now if we say, therefore, that man is not able to receive by faith itself the grace of Jesus Christ and that it is necessary that it is God by His own active virtue which produces internally the disposition in such a manner that man receives it (concerning how we speak of this is conforming to the customary style of Scripture),[1] this is not to say however that this impotence excused us before God and entirely removed or even diminishes the blame of this unbelief in order to exempt us from the merited punishment. Our inability does not come from the doctrine which is presented to us as being difficult to conceive. If we were commanded to find the hidden causes of the properties of a magnet or the proportion which exists between a circle and a square, or some other things which approach this degree of difficulty and which we might not be able to arrive at a suitable answer, we would cite their difficulty as an excuse and perhaps would attribute it to less equitable judgment. But the doctrine of salvation is easy to comprehend as well as evident. If God had not given us the faculties of understanding and of the will by which we are men, and being men capable of understanding that which one proposes to us which is intelligible concerning faith—such as to believe that which is founded in clear and manifest reasons, to love and desire good and desirable things, to flee from all that which is contrary to good in that which is proposed to us as being intelligible in itself, or in believing that which

---

1   Amyraut emphasizes here his own orthodoxy and declares that his terminology and thought process coheres with the traditional Orthodox view of how Scripture defines man's depravity and complete inability to be converted without the Spirit's regeneration. Hence, he uses the phrase to verify his perspective as being within the "normal style or sense of Scripture."

is founded in clear and apparent reasons, or of loving and desiring good and desirable things, and even those fleeting ones which are not—we would again claim this excuse and with good reason. The things destitute of this faculty have nothing to fear as a result of not having recognized the excellence of the gospel. But we have been endowed with these from the beginning and God has preserved them in us, our sin notwithstanding. Otherwise we would not be men. And although we have these faculties and although the doctrine of salvation is itself evident (Romans 1:91–20), if nevertheless we had not heard it spoken, as one who had been raised[1] in another world, based solely on our own ability, we would not be able to understand it as we should, as it is said, claiming the cause of ignorance. But concerning "their voice," says the Apostle of his companions and of himself, *"has it not gone out into all the earth"* (Romans 10:18)? Is there hardly any nation, then, which either has not heard the preaching of the gospel of Christ or which is not close to those in which it has been preached? And if there is someone among all the others who has not heard the gospel proclaimed and to which one cannot accuse that he has ignored the gospel in disdain or indifference, he will not be condemned because he has in fact despised the name of Christ, but because he would have reviled the voice of the heavens, and the cry of providence, and the very patience of God who calls all to repentance. In Scripture there is sufficient testimony that there is within lost man, whatever else there might be, a hardness of heart so invincible that even if Christ Himself had been proclaimed so boldly and clearly as He was in Jerusalem, he would have still despised Him. Because this impotence comes from the fact that we are now by nature wicked, that is, that the vice which is in us has spread its roots so deep and has so confirmed its habits, it has acquired for itself a domain so absolute and so possesses all the faculties of our souls, that not only would we not know how to break them if we truly wanted to, but that it is impossible that we could even desire to do so.[2] For our faculties are not only so debilitated by vice that, in the same manner, if they truly desired to do otherwise, their attempts would be lacking and their efforts failing, and by consequence, they would be unable even to break a more powerful habit. More so, these faculties are completely enslaved to sin and even dead in terms

---

1   *Nourri.*

2   Amyraut contends that even the philosophers themselves say that man is unable to break free from being his true self due to the very force of evil habits of the soul when they are firmly entrenched; Amyraut notes in the margin of his text: "Aristotle speaks this way about unjust men."

of good sentimentalities, so much so that it is impossible that they are even able to want anything else other than this powerful convention of sin which commands it. Now the stronger, the more profound, and inveterate such a disposition of the soul is, the more it is despised and wicked, and the more it merits blame. Thus, as for impotence of this kind excusing its unbelief, the greater it is the more it merits blame and punishment. Otherwise the demons would not deserve punishment[1] because they are not able to do other than sin; and to exempt oneself from blame and from the torment of sin, there would be no better reality than to make himself as despicable as the devil. Certainly, then, as virtue is incomparably more excellent when it has risen to such a point that it cannot be corrupted, as long as it is great and fully possess the soul, it is so much more praiseworthy when it proceeds from other virtues even more eminent and more perfect, like the virtue of the angels. So also is sin[2] which emanates to such a degree that it is totally incorrigible and is more worthy of hatred, and the actions which proceed from it are more worthy of punishment, as proceeding from a more profound and abominable perversity of the spirit.

---

1 *Supplice.*
2 Vice.

Chapter 9

The Election and Predestination of God by Which He Has Ordained to Accomplish Salvation in Some and Not in Others: Why Does This Occur?

[102] The nature of men being such, if God had had no other intention[1] in ordaining to send His Son to the world than to present Him as a Redeemer equally[2] and universally to all, even as great as this love is from which this counsel proceeded, it would have been useless to human kind and the sending and sufferings of His Son entirely disappointing. Thus, it being hardly in agreement with His wisdom to send His Son into the world and there suffer an ignominious death without producing any effect toward the salvation of men, and with His unspeakable mercy and love to allow the whole human race to perish in this condemnation, He did not withhold a means of attaining salvation; this was to deploy such an efficacy of His power in man that it would overcome all of the corruption within his understanding and his will so as to make him believe and embrace the grace which is offered to him. Thus, notwithstanding all the resistance that intellectual darkness and the perversity of the will carry, man would surrender nevertheless to the evidence of the truth, recognize the necessity and the excellence of this Redeemer, and seek in Him his own deliverance. It is therefore all within God's counsel, which constitutes what one calls election or predestination, and where God shows both His desire and the abundantly excelled riches of His mercy toward those whom He has elected and predestined in order to give faith to them, and His severity towards those whom He has abandoned

---

1 *N'eust pris autre conseil* ... "had not taken other counsel," or intention.
2 (1658) edition removes the word "equally" here as well.

to themselves, accomplishing both in His sovereign freedom the dispensation of this praiseworthy mystery.

[104] Concerning God's mercy, it appears here as surpassing[1] its own boundaries. For in His seeing the human race lying in such a miserable condition and having been touched by it, He shows a true demonstration of His nature inclined toward mercy. But to the extent that His justice, which demands retribution, restrains and hinders an intended mercy, it cannot be fruitful for us. Yet, because God is not content to be touched simply by some pity, but has sought in His wisdom the way to satisfy His justice—truly resolving to send His Son to the earth and to abandon Him to death on the cross for the universal salvation of the world—in this, He has shown an intense compassion which reinforces itself and, in a manner of speaking, overtakes the obstacles of His justice. Nevertheless this compassion still presupposes a faith-oriented condition suitable to man, that is, by faith alone in the Redeemer, which also demonstrates true repentance in man. Without this faith, God does not wish that His mercy should be of any use to us. And as there is some natural correspondence between the integrity of the creature and the goodness of the Creator, and as there is also some necessary relation between the corruption of man and the justice of the Judge of the world, so there seems to be some appropriate relation between genuine faith and repentance of the sinner with that of divine mercy. In this manner, one can explain it thus: God loves His creature to the extent that he is perfect;[2] God also punishes man to the extent that he is a sinner. Therefore, it can be stated also that God pardons the sinner to the extent that with genuine faith he has recourse to God's mercy. But far from the love of God being able to presuppose this condition in man, it is necessary to presuppose that it is not there, indeed even that it cannot be there unless God Himself creates it to be there by His power. Thus, God's mercy at this point exceeds all measure and all intelligence. And the Apostle seems to refer to this not only when he says that in this "*God is shown to be rich in mercy, that by His great love with which He has loved us, even when we were dead in our trespasses, He made us alive together with Christ*" (Ephesians 2:4–5), but also when he calls this sort of love, *foreknowledge*; thus, "*those whom God has foreknown, he has also predestined*"(Romans 8:29). And elsewhere, he states,

---

1 *Sortie* ... "leaving its boundaries."
2 Whole or complete, which man is not in his depraved state.

"*God has not forsaken His people whom He foreknew*" (Romans 11:2). Now while this word *to know* in the Scripture sometimes signifies *to love*—but to love nevertheless in consequence of the approbation of some quality or condition which is found in the thing that is loved and which invites these affections, as when it is said that "*God knows the way of the righteous*" (Psalms 1:6)—the foreknowledge spoken of here is a love which precedes every condition and all considerations of some lovable quality in the creature. And here one can recall the words of the Epistle to the Galatians that, "*When you did not know God, you served rather those which by nature are not gods, but now since you have known God, or rather YOU HAVE BEEN KNOWN BY GOD, why do you turn away backwards to the weak and worthless elemental things, which you wish to serve?*" (Galatians 4:8–9).[1] For although the word "to know" is simply employed here, this emphatic correction, however, and this opposition to the knowledge that the Galatians had of God, had a very great force and conveys as much as if it served for the word "foreknowledge." It is true that since this foreknowledge or God's love is the motive of our election and predestination to faith, and since predestination depends on it as a consequence, St. Peter takes it[2] for this particular predestination by which Christ was ordained to be sent to the earth for the redemption of the world. For he says that we have been redeemed from our vain way of life by the blood of Christ, as of the lamb without spot and without blemish: St Peter further states, "Christ was foreknown before the foundation of the world, but manifested to us in these last days" (1 Peter 1:20). But that does not remove from St. Paul the original significance of the word.

[108] Concerning God's justice, the severity of God appears also in this counsel in that He does not make this present grace universal as the other, but restricts it to some and leaves others to themselves. For unlike the preceding grace which regarded the whole human race in general, as we have deduced above, this one only regards one part only and leaves the other destitute. Moreover, those whom God elects and distinguishes from the others in this manner are a very small number, which caused Christ to observe that "*many are called, but few chosen.*"[3] It is also very true that where

---

1   Emphasis in capitalized letters original to Amyraut.
2   Amyraut parenthetically inserts here: "by a manner of speaking rather ordinarily in Scripture where that which follows is used for that which precedes it, and that which precedes it from what necessarily follows."
3   Matthew 22:14. Amyraut mistakenly cited Mt. 10:16.

God has offered the same Redeemer equally to all, providing that they receive Him, He also gives testimony to a great love as much to the one as to the other. And those that He has passed over[1] have no less reason than those whom He has elected to recognize His mercy towards them in this regard. If these do not receive this Redeemer, they should count that to their own hardness and obstinacy, and if by consequence of their unbelief they remain eternally lost, they cannot attribute it to anyone other than themselves. For as we will see below at more length, even if God is for some the cause of faith and salvation, He is not the cause of unbelief and subsequent damnation in the others. If His election is efficacious for some really and actually to accomplish the condition upon which salvation depends, the unbelief of the others does not come from divine reprobation, as the cause which activates it by its own efficacy, but from their own blindness and moral perversity.[2] But always in that He uses such mercy towards some in whom He wishes to overcome that blindness and perversity, and where He does not use it toward the others and especially in those He has given over to the hardness of their hearts in much greater number than the others, there is a just severity. It is for this reason that comes those thoughts in the spirit of man which the Apostle reports in the epistle of Romans stating, "*But you will say to me, 'why does He yet find fault? For who is able to resist His will?'*" (Romans 9:19); for St. Paul has already noted that, "*He has mercy upon whom He wishes, and hardens whom He wishes*" (Romans 9:18). And to which he responds with these words capable of rebutting the audacity of the flesh, that "*on the contrary, oh man, who are you who to argue against God? Will the thing formed say to the one who has formed it, 'Why have you made me in this way?' Doesn't the potter have the power to make from the same lump of clay one vessel for honor and another for dishonor?*" (Romans 9:20–21). In this Scripture, the Apostle notes that if the workers have the power to dispose of their material as it seems best to them because it is theirs, then the material they use to make the vessels for dishonor does not have any more merit than that of those which are destined

---

1   Delaissez.

2   Amyraut here argues that though God does predestine the elect to salvation through regeneration, God however does not demonstrate a double predestination or forced reprobation where as God forces the lost to remain in their unbelief or damns them preemptively so as they have no chance, ability, or opportunity to respond to the gospel. Rather, Amyraut states that God simply passes over the lost, the un-elect, and leaves them in their natural depraved state where as they would never willfully choose Christ in their own power.

for an honorable use. Rather, how much more does it concern the freedom within God's sovereignty, who as the Author of all things, and since the mass of humanity is universally corrupt, He takes one part of humanity in order to sanctify it while leaving the other in their natural rottenness, a rottenness which impedes men who are re-shaped by it to be able to be anything else other than stinking and infamous vessels.

[111] And it is to this freedom, as I have said before, that shows itself again in this matter. As such, that one can give some reason for the goodness which God shows to His creatures if they preserve the integrity from their origin—and the justice which He exercises over them when they degenerate from it, or even of the mercy that He grants them if they have recourse to it with assurance and repentance—Scripture itself does not reveal[1] the reasons for the dispensation of these things. Neither does Scripture teach us any reason for this choice which God makes of certain ones to enlarge the salutary gift of faith or of His having left other men behind in their condition, other than the free will of God. Otherwise God's action here might seem strange if man's misery is truly an object of compassion and all are equally miserable, and if the corruption of vice is an object of retribution, and all men are equally culpable. Nor, if you wanted to look elsewhere than in the Word of God, could you find any other reason than this same divine freewill.

So where else could you find a suitable answer? Could it be in our works which God has from all eternity foreseen that we would do? Certainly not![2] For all good works not only follow faith and do not precede it, according to the Apostle who states, *"that which is done without faith is sin"* (Romans 14:23), and that *"without faith it is impossible to please God"* (Hebrews 11:6), but works depend upon faith as the cause by which they are necessarily and uniquely produced. For this reason it is said that it is faith *"which purifies hearts"* (Acts 15:9). Therefore, before foreseeing the good works it is necessary to foresee the faith, and God cannot see the faith in us, unless He has first ordained to create it there Himself. Thus, the Apostle says that *"we are not saved because of works that we have done, but because God has saved us by grace through faith, so that we might do good works and might walk in them"* (Ephesians 2:6–7). Again elsewhere, he expressly states that, *"God has saved us and called us with a holy calling, not according to our works but according to His own covenant and that grace*

---

1 *Taise.*
2 *Nenny!* Equivalent to the Old English "nonny" as in "no," or may it never be!

which we have been given in Christ Jesus in eternity past" (2 Timothy 1:9). And in another scripture, introducing Jacob and Esau as an example of the grace which God shows to some in calling them efficaciously by virtue of His Spirit and in consequence of His election, while leaving others behind, God first chooses those who are extremely equal in their natural condition—i.e. children of the same father and the same mother, being conceived in the same womb and born at the same time. He then remarks that the one has been preferred to the other by divine prophecy, the younger to the older, *"who had yet done neither good nor evil,"* in order to show that in this economy of His grace, God has had no regard for their works and thus *'so that the purpose fixed according to the election of God might remain firm"* (Romans 9:10–12).

[113]   Could it therefore be in faith itself? Again, no indeed! Since faith does not come from ourselves, but is a gift of God. And before seeing any faith in us, God had ordained to put it there. And we search the reason why He had thus ordained faith this way. It appears that God had not ordained to give faith to all the world, since the Apostle states, for *"faith does not belong to all'* (2 Thessalonians 3:2). Otherwise all the world would believe, which is more than refuted by experience. For this reason in another place he calls faith *"the faith of the elect of God"* (Titus 1:1) to show that God, has in particular, elected some to give them this grace to believe. But this cannot be the same faith, as a thing foreknown and antecedent, which has moved Him to elect them to believe rather than the others.

[114]   Finally, could it therefore be because He has foreseen that they would use the saving grace which is offered to them in a better way than the others? To this question, also no! For the good use of saving grace consists either in it being embraced through faith or that in having been embraced it is made to bear fruit in good works. Since we have shown that this eternal decree to give faith cannot be founded on either foreseen faith or good works, it therefore necessarily follows that it cannot be founded upon God having foreseen the good use of that grace either.

[115]   However, what if someone wishes to go even deeper in this quest and attempt to distinguish subtly between the degrees of the efficacy which God deploys to convert men to salvation and to say that the last degrees have been added since the preceding ones had not been rejected, but had, on the contrary, been well used?[1] We will return the question by asking

---

1   Though cloaked in difficult phraseology, Amyraut here is answering the Arminian assertion

who could have induced God to give these first degrees of efficacy to some and to deny them to others who do not, nor will ever sense them; and why would God ordain that those who use these preceding degrees by which they have been created receive the others which follow, while so many others who could have received them equally have lost them through abuse or neglect? For, to resort here to the freedom of the will is a useless thing. From the perspective that God must have ordained to foresee the will of those individuals with His preceding gifts and not to foresee that of the others, and that the will of all men being equally enslaved to the corruption of sin, it is entirely unimaginable how it could have been equally foreseen in some and nevertheless the outcomes be dissimilar. It would have been necessary either for corruption to have destroyed[1] these first degrees of the grace of the Spirit in all of them—though nevertheless it appears that several actually believe—or not to have destroyed it in any of them; and nevertheless, it is presupposed that the outcomes are different. Or, perhaps God had ordained to cause in some that their corrupted will would not destroy these graces, allowing themselves to be overcome. Consequently, then, from what He has enacted in some, elsewhere, He has plainly not done it to others; thus, it is concerning this that we seek a reason and cannot find anything other than the free will of God Himself.

[116] Thus, the scriptures teach us. For after St. Paul has presented the beautiful picture of the different grace toward men in Jacob and Esau, he poses this question, "*What will we say therefore? Is there injustice in God?*" (Romans 9:14). For in light of the equality of these two children some find such a preferential choice strange. So he responds, "*May it never be! For he said to Moses "I will have mercy upon whom I will have mercy, and will be merciful to him to whom I will be merciful*" (Romans 9:14). This response not only would be unnecessary and inappropriate if one had been able find some distinction either in the works of men or in the disposition and freedom of their wills, but it also expresses with a marvelously evident energy that this thing depends absolutely upon God using His mercy with complete freedom, and that we

---

that God ultimately responds to man's own genuine faith, a faith which is common to man and which man may seemingly accept or reject at will. As such, Amyraut debunks here that God operates in such a way as to preferentiate those who actually "use well the preceding degrees," which means to respond preveniently to God's offer so that God would offer more effectual grace (or the "last degrees of grace") in conversion.

1 *Esteindre* ... "extinguish."

therefore cannot probe for any cause other than His will. It is not that God, who as being wise beyond all our comprehension, has made this choice of men unconfidently and turned them out of the fort into the wilderness, so to speak, and threw over them the random fate by which they might or might not perish. It does not even occur to us to have such thoughts. Regardless of what we attribute to the freedom of His good pleasure, we do not stop believing that it has proceeded from His ordinary wisdom. And St. Paul gives it to us thus, to believe when after having proposed so beautiful an example of the freedom of God in calling the Jews to be favored above all the nations of the world, then by rejecting these very same Jews and in the subsequent calling of the nations to a knowledge of Him, and finally in the reunion of these two peoples in the same Christ by the mercy that God will some day render to the posterity of Abraham, he writes, "*Oh, the depth of the riches and of the wisdom and of the knowledge of God!*" (Romans 11:33). Thus, he shows that this is not done apart from God having exercised His wisdom in it. But we wish to declare that there is no cause in men for this diversity of God's favor toward them and that He has not revealed to us any other cause than His will alone. This is so that we who believe might be entirely beholden for our salvation to His mercy; so that those who do not believe might attribute it to the hardness of their hearts; and further, so that those who seek out the causes why these have believed rather than those, why those have been rejected rather than these, might respect the secrets of God whom they are not able to fathom and might recognize that He is sovereignly free in the dispensation of His graces.

Chapter 10

That According to this Doctrine, God Cannot Be Accused of Being a "Respecter of Persons," or of Being the Author of Sin, or the Cause of Man's Lostness.

[119] These things being explained in this way, I do not think that there is anyone who would want to object, as it is customary to do against the idea of predestination, to impose upon God that He esteems the appearance of men, or that He is the author of sin, or that with cruelty unworthy of the excellence of His nature, He has willed as with a joyful[1] heart to display His glory in the eternal damnation of humans. For which of these criticisms going forward is He able to own?[2] Certainly the preference for persons is a vice only when it is a question of comparison between two men and of their causes or of their action; an unjust judge of their quarrel regards not the nature of the action or the cause of which they plead, in order to render justice for the one whom it pertains, but to some condition such as riches, power, beauty, or some other thing which does not pertain to the case, and which solicits favor for one above the other. So much so that the one who wins his case, wins it not because he is more worthy than that of his opponent, but because he is richer and because the judge trusts him; or he attains it because he is powerful and the judge fears him, or even because he is poor and the judge has pity upon him. Now God, desiring that justice be administered by the single consideration of what is just, unmixed with any passion which we experience, forbade among the people of Israel that

---

1 *Gayeté*.
2 *Quelle couleur desormais y peut-il avoir en ces blames?* ... lit. "which color is He able to have in these accusations?"

one have regard for the person of the poor in judgment (Exodus 23:3). Thus, it happens either that justice truly prevails,[1] but nevertheless this not out of his best judgment[2] but through his favor; or that the wrong remains victorious and justice is oppressed; this is by far more common. Now these things have no place here.

[121] For as we have described the nature of men above there is complete equality among them. They have all come from the hand of the same Author, who recognizes them equally as his work. They have all fallen into the same misery through the same sin by the rebellion[3] of the first man. Even in their nature they are equally corrupt and consequently equally guilty. This corruption is neither more profound, nor more firmly engrained, nor more invincible in one than the other. It is a leprosy in us which is equally incurable in all. What condition or quality therefore could there have been in one which appealed to the favor of God which could not also be found in the others? Concerning man's virtue, there was not a fiber or even an appearance of it in any of them. Concerning beauty, or riches, or power, or other similar qualities, there was none to be found; and even if there had been, these are not things which could enter into consideration with God in an action of this nature. As for the perversion of justice which ordinarily follows the esteem of persons in judgment, is there even a shadow of doubt here? Seeing that what God gives to some is out of His pure liberality and that which He refuses others, is there any law either in heaven or earth which commands that He give it to them? Also, if He consults His justice alone, would it not require that He absolutely deny it to them? Since God is the righteous judge of the universe all men stand as criminals in His presence. However, it pleases God to display His mercy in pardoning some and in punishing others as their crime deserves. If there were anything blameworthy in that it would not be that God punishes these, but that He does not punish all those; and thus He would not be caught because He had executed His justice upon some, but because in prejudicing His justice which requires that all be punished, He allowed Himself to be softened by His mercy toward others, which appears to come to be blamed when crimes find impunity. But God has remedied this and found in His wisdom the means to make way for His mercy without

---

1 L'emporte à la verité.
2 Pure consideration.
3 Revolte.

damaging His justice. He offers therefore grace to all these criminals equally, requiring of them only that they do not refuse it or demonstrate themselves to be unworthy of it, no matter how favorable their judgment in their own action which they adjudicate here. Or concerning God, is He required by some law, either in His nature or elsewhere, to offer this remission to them? Or if they refuse it, are they not worthy of all sorts of punishments? Yet, they all refuse it with an equal obstinacy and outrageously trample it under foot, where upon He exceeds all the measures of His mercy toward them for good in softening their hearts and directing them to their own well-being, and by a just severity abandoning the others to the hardness of their souls. Has therefore the faith of the first diminished the blameworthiness of the unbelief of the others? Or concerning the abundance of God's grace toward some in giving them faith, has it given the others the right to complain that God has not given it to them equally? Certainly there is no man who does not consider himself free in the distribution of his goods, to use them as seems good to him, even though there may exist between all men a human bond,[1] and even though we have no reason for offense or ill will against those who ask them of us. Yet, here where there is no such relationship between God and man and where there is a matter of relentless[2] wrath because of our iniquities, will we still complain if He does not remove all the limits on His mercy to our own fancy?

[124] As for God being author of sin, there is still less occasion to accuse Him. For of what sin would it be? That of the first man? No. We have shown above that it should be imputed solely to the temptation by Satan and to the man who allowed himself to be so seduced. Nor was it the decree[3] of God to not prohibit the operation of both temptation and sin; nor was it the certain and unquestionable foreknowledge of the outcome founded within this decree that He had not deployed any efficacy there. Would it be for this corruption which has since overrun the whole human race, the dominion of which we are under at birth? Not at all. For even as the first man was allowed to fall without God having pushed him toward it, man has produced his own contaminated children with the same corruption as he without God having any part in the communication or propagation of this stain. All that

---

1 *Une estoitte communion de sang* ... lit. "a narrow blood communion."
2 *Implacable.*
3 *Arrest.*

the providence of God does in this is to bless the seed of men to multiply, form, and fashion them with a remarkable artfulness, preserve them from all evil accidents, and then after having favored them with birth, He takes care for their education and their nourishment. With respect to sin, it passes from the fathers to the children without His hand intervening in some way.

Would it be, then, linked to man's sins which necessarily ensue and which render more and more this natural corruption incorrigible by practice? Again the same, no. Rather, man being an active creature by nature, to the extent that his faculties can disentangle themselves from the childishness and the impediment that the imperfections of the organs of his body imparts to them, so he also behaves how each of these leads him—the understanding to conceive, the emotion and will to either desire or avoid things. Now the vice with which these faculties are saturated accompanies them in their actions and penetrates them more and more without the providence of God contributing to it. If God preserves their lives, if He maintains their faculties, if He gives each of them strength in order to act according their natural condition, if He offers them the objects which they abuse instead of using properly as they should, not only does He not do them any harm, but whether in all or in part of these things, He actually manifests to them undeserved goodness, of which their un-acknowledgement is plainly a very punishable ingratitude.

Would it be in man's very act of unbelief, as one speaks, by which they reject the grace He offers to them? Still no. For if He does not give them belief, this is not the same as saying that He gives to them unbelief. If, as I say, God does not engender faith in them, it does not follow that He engenders the contrary. It is indeed the sun that illumines the earth, but the sun does not also render darkness. Darkness itself is naturally opaque. It is the sun moreover which warms the earth by the intervention of its light, but it is not the thing which by recoiling in winter causes it to be horribly cold. Coldness itself has that property and is worsened by the prevailing winds. If therefore the understanding of man to which the grace of Christ is offered through the gospel remains in darkness nonetheless, and if man's heart remains hard as rock or as cold as ice, concerning his possible salvation, that should be imputed to his own constitution of which he himself is author, and to the evil temptations which find his evil constitution vulnerable. Would it therefore finally be that in refusing the grace of Christ he becomes more hardened than he was before and even more incorrigible still in his evil, if he was even able to add anything to the hardness of his previous condition? Certainly as heavy objects naturally tend to fall, the more they fall and approach the ground, so to speak, the more their movement becomes violent; and as the corruption of man tends naturally toward sin, the more often it leads him the more this corruption takes root and these inclinations become violent, which is called hardening. But as heavy objects have this inclination of falling toward the ground from nothing other than their own nature, so the corruption of man has this momentum toward evil from nothing other than its own nature. Thus, all that the providence of God does in punishing this great ingratitude and obstinacy in man, is that He leaves, as says the Apostle, men to their own passions, which carry them away to all kinds of infamous actions, and hands the bridle to Satan, who coming to interject his temptations and effectively corrupt these rebellious children hollows out the eyes of their understanding and destroys in them all faculties which distinguish between good and evil. This, then, sadly extinguishes the small remnant of natural light that God has allowed since man's fall to keep the conservation of human society in the human conscience. For this reason it is also often said that God Himself hardens them, not because He adds to their wickedness, but because He does not remove it. Further, the passions of men do not come to such a horrible conclusion nor can the devil achieve such an absolute rule in men's hearts without some effect of His righteous providence.

[129] Now if God cannot be accused of being the author of man's sin, neither can it be imputed to Him that He is the cause of man's perdition. For the perdition of man consists in suffering punishment and since all punishment necessarily assumes a relationship to the crime in consequence of which it comes, and as the cause which merited it, what will impute to man his condemnation but his own sin? The criminals, who are evidently convicted of that which they have been accused, would they be well founded to name the causes of their torments as the magistrates who inflict judgment upon them? For we have seen to what God had destined man in His first creation and, very far from having some vein of cruelty in it, it can only be described as a marvelous goodness. And having still seen what God has done to lift man out of his condemnation, one can only describe it as a renowned and inestimable mercy. Having fallen from the enjoyment of this goodness by his own sin, and having despised this mercy in his evil obstinacy, the punishment which follows can have no other name than justice; this is also an exact justice to be marveled and is so much more exempt from all

blame, that God only employed it after the fall in order to avenge the scorn that man has shown toward this mercy. Similarly, men are accustomed to name in their magistrates such justice which punishes true crime a virtue, and they even praise them for it. If men direct praise toward these lesser magistrates on the earth, how can they turn and blame the universal Judge of the world? Although God did not have in the creation of man any other goal than to testify of His goodness in the work of redemption and to render toward man an incomparable mercy, it resulted nevertheless in the glory of His justice through man's punishment which makes a contempt of both, and so much so, that He can never be accused of having been excessively rigorous in the exercise of His justice, or too stingy and defective in the dispensation of His grace.

CHAPTER 11

HOW ONE DISCERNS THE MEANS BY WHICH GOD ACCOMPLISHES THIS CONDITION OF FAITH IN HIS ELECT AND RENDERS HIS PREDESTINATION AS A CERTAIN AND INFALLIBLE REALITY

[131] The counsels[1] of God that one calls conditional—a counsel being that which God has ordained to do something—and by conditional meaning that His creatures execute such and such commandments and are so decreed that the outcome of them depends upon the execution or non-execution of the given condition. Such is the conditional decree by which He ordained to render the happiness of the first man perpetual, this is, if man continued to persevere in his integrity. So also was that counsel conditional by which He decreed to give the people of Israel a perfectly happy life in the land of Canaan, that is, if they had completely observed the law that He had given. Also by this conditional decree He has ordained to save all men by our Lord Jesus, that is, if they do not show themselves to be unworthy through unbelief. Therefore in these kinds of conditional counsels[2], the certainty of the execution of the condition is tied necessarily to the certainty of the outcome of the counsels themselves. And by the same means the knowledge that one might have of the certainty of the one depends upon his knowledge of the other. Because, as we have said above, God certainly knew the faculties of man and knew exactly to what extent they would resist temptation to evil; He also certainly knew that man would fall from his integrity, therefore the conditional counsel of man's perpetual blessing was never to take place. The corruption of sin having then expanded over the whole human race and the

---

1 (1658) edition: dispositions or wills.
2 (1658) edition: "Therefore in this type of disposition of the will of God, ... "

law requiring a perfect holiness, God also saw that it was impossible that Israel fulfill the law, securing therefore that this conditional counsel concerning the happiness of Canaan never succeed. And this corruption having already so spread in man that it has infected the deepest part of his faculties, and has rendered him entirely incapable to believe in the Redeemer—that is unless God himself forms faith in his heart—God foreknows certainly and undoubtedly who will be saved because He has resolved to give them belief, and He knows who will not believe because He has ordained not to give faith in the same way for them.

[133] Thus, in regard to God, the knowledge of the outcome is clear and infallible. With respect to men it is otherwise. If God was content to offer the grace of salvation only externally, considering the condition in which we are all born, it would be easy to predict that it would be universally rejected. Similarly, it is not difficult to say that the sun would not be known in a land where all that inhabitants are blind. But because God has elected some and passed over others, and because He has not revealed to us who these are in particular or shown their names written in His register, no one can be completely assured that even his neighbor is saved, in so far as he does not know if he himself is among those to whom it will be given to truly believe. This follows the statement of the Apostle, that '*God knows those who are His*' (2 Timothy 2:19).

[134] As for those counsels that one commonly calls absolute, that is, by which God, moved by His pure will, resolved to do something without having regard to any such condition, the outcome is indubitably absolute. And God knows all that will take place, not because such and such a condition should certainly precede it, but because He has resolutely determined to do it. But the certainty which men have of it can depend upon nothing other than two things:

[135] The first is the consideration of the outcome itself, when it has really and in fact taken place. For if we see something accomplished[1] that only God could do, it must be necessarily concluded that since it is done, God had ordained that it would be done. For all that is done by the operation of His power, maintaining that time has flowed since the creation of the world, had been ordained before the world was, from all eternity. From this reality of the absolute counsel, each faithful believer knows he has been elected

---

1 *Fait* ... "done or made."

from the beginning to have faith, because he has felt it in himself, because it has illumined a light in his understanding, because it has engendered peace in his conscience, and because it has begun a sanctification in his will and affections which could not have come from any other cause than the divine goodness and power. Concerning the manner whereby one happens to compare the sentiments of his soul with the description of faith and its effects in the elect found in Holy Scripture, he should not doubt at all that he is among the number of the elect in view of the conformity that he recognizes between the Word of God at this point and the movements and sentiments of his own soul.

[136] The second is the revelation that God makes of His decree and the judgment of His will in this regard. For since in God as in other intelligent causes the concurrence of just two things is necessary in order to produce an effect, namely power and will— knowing that God is endowed with infinite power, if we are assured by Him concerning His will, the certainty of the outcome is entirely beyond doubt. Thus, although we may not know who in particular among men is or is not of the elect or who among men truly believes and who does not believe—except only God and the heart of man which judge the truth and sincerity of the movement of man's own conscience—we are plainly assured that there are some who truly believe in the same way that God has revealed to us in His word that He has truly elected some to believe. And while we may be entirely ignorant of the manner in which this occurs, we ought not for this reason be less assured of both the truth of the action of God which leads His counsel to execution and the infallible outcome which results from it.

[137] In fact, how many things are there concerning the mind and movement of God of which we are truly ignorant as to *why* and *how*, which are not able to be understood, and which we do not any longer doubt as being true? Such as things either important to life or even in what does life itself consists? For who is there among us who has exactly understood either the harmony of all the parts and faculties of the body together in the functions of life which we have in common with the animals, or the nature of the dominion that the superior faculties of our souls have over those of the body, or the exercise of these things in commanding on the one hand and obeying on the other? Or what is the nature of the actions of our spirits, as they go about in the contemplation and comprehension of objects which are shown to them, or as they turn to reflect upon themselves in order to understand

themselves and the means of their own intelligence? Certainly the meaning of these things will be found, if we wish to notice, in the distribution of the nourishment in our bodies necessary for the strength and sustenance for the vital movements of our heart and our lungs, the functions of the senses of the body and especially the eyes, the movements of the members which obey those of the understanding (mind) and will, the operation of the mind and the will themselves, and to the activities so hidden, the things so abstruse and so profound that because of their subtlety, they discourage knowledge of them so that they will never be completely understood. Very often, the more subtly men discuss such matters the more they obscure them and do not even understand it themselves. And nevertheless we do not doubt at all that each of these things exist, and having had the sense to call out those who have otherwise called into doubt the truth of these things, we accuse them in all fairness. If we had therefore no other instruction of this operation of God in us than the feeling of its efficacy, this would be enough to content us and to console our consciences. And do not doubt the joy that a dead man would have in seeing himself raised from the tomb by the power of God, such as the poor man Lazarus, that it would be any less sensible for not knowing *how* God restored and relit the natural warmth in him by which we see, and how God rejoined his soul to his body to animate it anew so as to perform all the functions of life by His intervention.

[139] Nevertheless, if we will consider carefully both the Word of God and the nature of man, it will be easy to gather from the comparison of one with the other, at least as much as it should be known to us, in what fashion God acts in men to lead toward His result to grant us belief.[1] For to believe, as everyone is able to understand it, is nothing but to be persuaded of the truth of something. And in order to be worthy of the excellence of man's nature, this persuasion ought to be accompanied, indeed to originate from the knowledge of the nature of the thing that is believed. Because man does not have a brute nature, but is endowed with understanding, he consequently ought to act according to the knowledge which it has of things. If therefore the thing which is presented to our understanding is such that there is nothing left to seek but its truthfulness alone, and to make him content for having understood it, the understanding of man ought to acquiesce in the comprehension of the truth when he has clearly perceived it. Just as when

---

1 Belief in God and His gift of saving faith.

one has found the proof[1] of some beautiful geometric question, or the clear and pertinent reason for some stunning effect of nature, or for other things which lie in contemplation only, the evidence of the truth is available to the one who is seeking. If the thing that is proposed to us is such that it is beyond the knowledge of the truth, and one still fails to seek the beauty of honesty and of virtue and usefulness—joined with the sweetness of enjoyment— one should not be content with the simple and bare knowledge of what is basically true, but one should be moved by the love of that which is honest and beautiful, and touched with the desire for the enjoyment of that which is suitably and proportionately useful according to its own excellence.

[140]   For example, if one presents to a man who is pressed by financial necessity a gift, or to someone who is threatened by sickness a beneficial medication, the one could not have a true knowledge of his poverty or the quality of the treasure which had been given to him, nor could the other have the true knowledge of his sickness or the peril which he is in, nor of the virtue of the medication secured for him in it, if he has not instantly conceded to receive it. If he refuses it, he must be ignoring his poverty or the richness of the gift, or he must be ignoring his sickness or the excellence of the medication. But what if the man to whom this treasure was offered had the sentiment of the ancient philosophers who despised gold and silver and did not follow suit? It would signify that either he does not think himself to be poor and that he despises the means of his enrichment, or that if he does think himself to be poor, it is a poverty which gold and silver cannot remedy. The void of his necessity must be filled by some other thing, perhaps such as the knowledge of the arts and sciences. If the sick man refuses the medication, or if he despises medicine in general, it would be a sign that he does not believe that medicine has such virtue attributed to it; or perhaps it is simply because of his queasiness of the bad taste or the nausea that he fears will accompany it, or worse still, perhaps it is because he does not believe that he is truly sick or is not concerned about death. Yet, it might be because he does not esteem that life is so desirable or death so fearful, that in consideration of them, he fails to subject himself to the bitterness of the cures. Thus, the refusal of either of the reasons results from a deprived estimate which does not attribute to these things their just worth and by consequence, is not a true knowledge.

---

1   *La demonstration.*

[142] God therefore acts in two ways toward us to cause us to believe in Christ as Savior and Redeemer of the world. On the one hand He causes us to preach His gospel, as a doctrine of heavenly truth which surpasses in this respect not only all other religions, which can be nothing else but false, but also all human sciences and whatever truth they may contain. And not only this, but as the rule of piety and of virtue so typical to the excellence of the human nature that it alone cannot only give it a relative perfection of the faculties of the understanding and the will by which it excels above all animals, but even bring it to a point which far surpasses its natural condition and the state of its first origin. And finally, as the height of our happiness, and the sole means, I declare, to attain the happiest and glorious immortality, is found according to that Scripture that *"this is eternal life to know the one true God and that He has sent Jesus Christ"* (John 17:3). On the other hand, because all the faculties of our souls are so corrupted and saturated with sin even to their greatest depths—that they are totally incapable of perceiving the foundations so that they are also totally incapable of perceiving the truth and excellence of these things, God acts in such a manner in our minds by His internal virtue, that He expelled the vice and the darkness and allows them to see the misery of the condition in which they were born, and that it is contrary to the excellence of that to which the gospel calls them. God also conveys the contrast between their natural ignorance and the light of His truth, between their natural corruption and the excellence of His purity and holiness, and finally between the curse under which we naturally lie and the height of His eternal happiness.

[144] The discussion being proposed in this way and our interior faculties being so well disposed by the grace of God, it is impossible from now on that we would not believe. That is, that it would be impossible that we receive the light of this truth and then not desire ardently to possess as much the holiness that it communicates, as the happiness which it offers. By this means the outcome of this counsel of God is indubitable. Thus, St. Paul manifestly testifies to this when he does not ask anything for the Ephesians in his prayer except that *"the God of our Savior Jesus Christ, the Father of glory, might give them the spirit of wisdom and of revelation through the knowledge of Himself, that the eyes of their understanding might be illumined that they might know what is the hope of His calling and what are the riches of the glory of His inheritance in the saints and what it is the exceeding greatness of His power toward us who believe"* (Ephesians 1:17–19). For he was persuaded that if they knew this

and if they had their understanding so well disposed that they were capable of clear and certain understanding, all their affections would be enamored and their wills necessarily determined to follow these things. And elsewhere he desires that *"they might be able to comprehend with all the saints what is the breadth, the depth and the height of the love of Christ which surpasses all knowledge, so that they might be filled up with all the fullness of God"* (Ephesians 3:18–19). For it is the knowledge of the love of Christ which carries with faith all the fullness of Christian virtue. And it is this of which Christ Himself spoke, that after having given these words from Isaiah, *"and they will be all taught by God,"* He adds, *"whoever has heard and has learned from the Father comes to me"* (John 6:45). As He wanted to emphasize, that to come to Him is to believe in Him, and in order to participate in the salvation of which He is Author to all who believe, it is necessary only *"to be taught by God and to learn"* that the knowledge God gives of the excellence of things that He presents in His gospel, including after faith all that is necessary to salvation and to life, knowledge, I say, which arises from the power of the Spirit that is invested with all efficacy. In fact, since the matter of faith is very difficult because of the hardness of our hearts and the resistance which our flesh presents to these things, though its fulfillment is certain, all reluctance being constrained to yield before this power, the Apostle uses these words in place of those given above, that *"we believe according to His incomparably great power. That power is the same as the mighty strength He exerted when He raised Christ from the dead and seated Him at his right hand in the heavenly realms"* (Ephesians 1:19–20). For would there be need of such power if it was a question of only a common result?[1] And where such a power is deployed, could anyone resist that would make the outcome doubtful, or who could prevail against it? Nevertheless, because this is done by the intervention of the knowledge of the excellence of the gospel in all of the considerations of which it has been made mention, the same St. Paul says that his preaching, which takes captive the thoughts of men into obedience of Christ, is with *'demonstration of the Spirit and the power'* (1 Corinthians 2:4), making use of a phrase which signifies for these reasons that the truth is so evident that it forces the understanding to receive it and overcomes all resistance. Thus, God who has ordained to give faith to His elect, executes this decree in a fashion which in no way makes its

---

1 *Un effect vulgaire.*

outcome doubtful and assures by this means the salvation of those who are part of this eternal election.

Chapter 12

That in the Process of Predestination God Does Not Destroy the Nature of Man's Free Will

[147] It is true that there are many that find what seems to them to be a great difficulty in this doctrine. That is, that man having been created with a rational nature and consequently free in his actions, it does not seem consistent with the goodness and wisdom of God to act in him in any other way than in accord with and in proportion to his nature. If therefore, they say, the outcome of this action is certain and inevitable and if it is necessary that one in whom God acts in this way must believe, there does not remain any freedom of will in him. And conversely, if there is true freedom of will in man, they surmise the outcome of salvation must be in doubt and consequently election itself is uncertain and mutable. Now I do not think it is even necessary for Christians to inquire as to the nature of the will of man and its freedom, providing that they have perceived by experience such efficacy of the grace of God in themselves, not only that they might believe in Christ, but that it is even impossible for them not to believe. For what interest do we have in the conservation of this freedom, if its effect is to keep us in such a state that we might be inclined to reject Jesus Christ as much as to receive Him, or to deprive ourselves of salvation as much as to embrace it when the gospel is presented to us?[1] Certainly if this condition of being saved, indeed of being placed in such a state that it is impossible that we could not be saved, could only be acquired through the loss of our

---

1 Amyraut here asks the principle question in terms of man's free will and human ability. He questions if it is indeed worth for man to retain his seemingly "unlimited" freedom intact, which is actually a fallen and depraved "free" will and which can only freely lead man into open sin, rebellion, and death or rather, to submit man's limited freedom to God's providence, restoration, and gain eternal life—which is the truest freedom in God's presence.

freedom, we would render it over cheerfully and even desire to be deprived of it if only to make the hope of our salvation sure and to make it absolutely certain and its fulfillment unquestionable.

[49] For the certainty of the favor of a prince is ordinarily accompanied by prosperity and greatness. Therefore if there was someone who was so much in the good grace of his prince that the continuance of his good fortune depended solely upon his own faithfulness and the perseverance of his will in the love that he has for his sovereign, could it also be presumed that he would wish to be reduced to a state in which he would be unable to someday hate his prince and thus fall from his favor and from the good fortune that he possesses in it, and in which he could never do anything but ardently love his sovereign—in part because this is his desire and in part because this is also his good fortune? And if he could purchase this assurance at the price of the freedom of his will, is it imaginable that he would complain at all about the so called loss? Truly, in conserving this claimed freedom of the will which makes him equally capable of the one as of the other, nothing could occur but one of these two outcomes: either that he will persevere in the love of his price and so will determine the freedom of his will in the direction of his well-being, or he will turn the love that he has for his prince into hate and his good fortune into evil. For it is hardly conceivable that he would remain forever in the balance of indecision. The first outcome he should desire and the second he should abhor and fear. If therefore he could lose his freedom of will so as to remain inseparably attached to the love and the benevolence of his prince, it would only occur to him that he should ardently desire this. If he keeps this claimed freedom he has no advantage, even providing he remains in indecision if that were even possible, except seeing himself perpetually in peril of this which he should abhor and fear above all things. And if he completely determines himself to that course, the advantage which returns to him is a most atrocious crime that he commits and his ruin from top to bottom.

[151] But why merely call this a peril? In the thing which is now in question, the evil is at every point inevitable. For if Adam in his integrity, having such a perfect constitution with respect to his faculties, experimented to such a degree to his own great demise[1] and that of the whole human race in consequence of having of mutable condition, what should we expect from

---

1 Evil.

the corruption which has befallen our spirits through his sin and especially toward the range of temptations to which we are subject as part of the world and from the devil? It would therefore be much better for us to lose this freedom if we have it and to assure by this means the hope of our salvation, than for us to conserve for ourselves, with such a manifest and inevitable peril, the power to lose it. More so, it is not necessary to fear that our nature has degenerated in any degree from its excellence. For if the perfection of our nature consists in piety and virtue, as we have briefly shown above, the greater and more deeply these good qualities are rooted in us, the further we will have come toward attaining perfection and the more firm and lasting these qualities will be in us. So then if they have been rendered entirely immutable, in the losing of this freedom of our will—if we indeed ever had such a freedom—so that we might be eternally constant and immutable in piety and in virtue, we would have indeed lost something of our natural condition, yet this would only be a perilous and temporary infirmity in order to acquire a higher degree of perfection and spiritual excellence. And the examples of the angels and of the future state of our glorification manifestly demonstrate this. For no one doubts that the angels are presently in a state of not being able to sin, and that we, when we have been received in heaven, will be in a very similar condition. Have the angels therefore lost some freedom of their will through the grace of their confirmation, or are we to lose it by our future glorification? If this is so, it is to acquire a much better and incomparably more desirable condition. Therefore the sooner we suffer this change the better. The sooner we lose this freedom, the more we ought to render thanks to God and to bless the preaching of the doctrine of the faith and the efficacy of the Spirit which has taken it away from us.

[153] But perhaps while it might be thus expedient for us, it is nevertheless not fitting for the wisdom of God to act otherwise in His creatures than in a fashion suitable to their nature. Let it be so. But since we see that this is for our well being and since He declares to us that such is His good will toward us, is it proper for us to inquire if the manner in which He wishes to execute it is or is not in accord with His wisdom? Are we so presumptuous, we who have not even seen the edges of His wisdom, to imagine that we are able to sound the depths of His wisdom? He who formed us as a clay pot makes all vessels and knows well the handles by which He must hold us. He who has given us the faculties we exercise also knows their limits so much better than we because He has placed them there, and He knows well that which

can start or stop, or arouse their movements, and which are the means of releasing or holding them. And if there, in heaven, He finds the necessary elements to keep spirits happy which are sanctified and the angels inseparably devoted to their well being, in what manner could it be remotely possible that they could take it away without simultaneously disparaging the leading of His wisdom? Then He also knows well how to provide for us down here and to harmonize the solidity of His election with the fragile nature of our faculties, without diminishing anything from the glory of His knowledge. In these depths, then, let us see if the operation of the Spirit of God on this point is in any way poorly suitable?

[154] First, when God moves within us this way He neither renders us blind to our own sentiments, as in the things which lack feelings, nor rough or unthoughtful as with the animals. For is it not men who believe in Christ, or in the same way believe that gravity exists,[1] or that light objects can fly, or rather do men carry themselves in the same manner in which beasts are led by their sensualities and appetites which excite them without rules or moderation, or without discourse or reason? If the operation of God's Spirit within us is reduced to that state, we could complain among us of a true change in our nature. But since neither piety nor virtue would be found among us, if that were possible, in what would our sovereign perfection be comprised? For neither do the beasts enjoy true contentment as if they possessed some treasure; nor do they think of the flowers of the earth and the stars in heaven, or of the joys of music and the harmony of the instruments, or of the knowledge found within studying the sciences. If we were like them, then we would not feel our own happiness either. Nevertheless, it is from our feelings deep within us in which lies the sweetness of joy. But far from the power of the Spirit moving us in this brute fashion, on the contrary, it improves our understanding and the faculties by which we are men, giving us knowledge and glimmers of insight concerning both ourselves and the grace of God toward us, insight which would have never otherwise entered our thoughts. This is why this spirit is given the name "*the Spirit of wisdom and of revelation*" (Ephesians 1:17),[2] whereas those who are destitute of it are

---

1 Though Newton's formula for Universal Gravitation would not be enunciated by him for another fifty-two years, Amyraut has a firm scientific grasp on describing objects which are heavy tend to always "fall to the center of the earth or ground." Thus, here the choice of the word "gravity" is anachronistic, yet it concisely says in one word where Amyraut took six.

2 Cf. also Proverbs 1:22.

said to be *fools*, having *"the eyes of their understanding yet walking in darkness"* (2 Corinthians 4:4).¹

[156] And though the Spirit efficaciously exercises His will in us, He does not, however, constrain us nor violate us. For constraint negatively acts against one's will. But who has ever heard it said of a man either that he believes something in spite of himself or that he loves something against his will? Belief is a persuasion. And one does not persuade a person by force. It is rational arguments that induce men to receive some truth, not constraint or violence. More so, love is a movement of both the emotion and will. To love, therefore, is either to desire good for the one whom we love or to wish good toward ourselves through this pleasure. Now it cannot be imagined that the will could desire something contrary to itself, or consequently that it love something while being constrained to do so by force. Therefore, the fact that we receive the truth of the gospel can be attributed to our perceiving it and it being natural to man that the understanding which clearly and certainly perceives a given truth acquiesces to it. And that we love the Spirit's movement in us is because we recognize its natural excellence and its utility, since it is natural for man to love ardently that which is reasonable and useful, if he truly recognizes it and experiences it as such.² Finally, if we consider the thing as we should, we will find that this operation of the Spirit in us is marvelously suited to our nature and consequently to the divine wisdom itself. God moves our emotions and our will through the agency of our understanding, and this is in accord with our nature. For is it not clear that these inferior faculties depend upon the superior one and follow its movement? And who is there among men who cannot cite some reason for what he is doing and who would not confess that he is led to do it for that reason? Do not those who say that the will sometimes acts contrary to the understanding, so as to demonstrate its freedom, perceive that in so speaking they themselves are actually assigning to this action of the will a reason which desires to show its freedom? Such a reason, in that it is a reason, can only have force in the will when it has first entered into the

---

1   Cf. also 1 John 1:6.
2   Here, Amyraut affirms that God does not force man to love Him nor does He violate man's will in saving him. Rather, God is merciful in showing man his need for salvation as His Spirit regenerates man to eternal life and enlightens his mind to this reality. Those who are not drawn by God's Spirit for salvation would only otherwise freely choose self and sin, and would only perpetually rebel against God's love in their natural state of depravity.

understanding; the understanding then judges what is expedient and what is not and if it must demonstrate its freedom or not and then, determining it and resolving the matter, leads the will in that direction and makes it unavoidably follow. Therefore, as in a machine where one wheel necessary depends upon another and this wheel upon the movement of a mainspring, it is normal action to roll the wheel by the mainspring which interlocks with it directly and by the interlocking cogs, to move the other. Similarly, in the beautiful arrangement of our faculties where corporal things depend upon the will and the will depends upon the understanding, it is well suited to our nature that God moves our will by exciting our emotions,[1] and our corporal actions by the means of our will, and the will by the intervention of our understanding.

[159] More so, God moves our understanding through knowledge of truth, excellence, and incomparable utility of the gospel. This again is suitable to their condition. For is there anything which could be more in accordance with their nature than the knowledge of these qualities? Or is there even anything which comes close to them which is not of this nature? When all the things which are capable of arresting the attention of our spirits and inducing us to certain actions, great and small, they will all be reduced into one of these categories—either true, honest, or delightful, or they are either virtuous and useful in some respect. Therefore the most suitable way that God can act in our understanding is to either present to it these things individually or even make it perceive them all together at one time. And this is what He does in the preaching of the gospel where these qualities all occur in a single subject, indeed to a supreme degree which exceeds infinitely their measure in all other things. God opens our understanding and drives from it its natural darkness, so that we are able to recognize clearly all these things in salvation which are offered to us, and He works in it such an efficacy that it is impossible either for us not to perceive them or for us not to yield to them, regardless of any resistance that our emotions or our carnal reason might at first offer.[2] This is again suitable to the nature of our spirits, which, the more excellent they

---

1 Affections.

2 Though described here in a more one-dimensional element than in his other works, Amyraut takes seriously the biblical prescription of conversion through the renewing of one's mind (Romans 12:2; Ephesians 4:3; Titus 3:5) and details the conversion experience through God's regeneration of the understanding (mind) as the principle mechanism which then leads man's emotion and ultimately his own will to choose Christ.

are the more necessarily and inevitably they feel within themselves and even beyond themselves, the power and efficacy of these things.

[160] For it is true, as even the philosophers themselves have recognized, that man's supreme good consists in virtue and in happiness which lacks in nothing, and that men naturally and necessarily seek their own supreme good in all things, whether good or evil, by which their understanding construes it to be to them; thus, it cannot be that in the gospel offer to us through Christ—which is a supreme good that infinitely excels all that the philosophers have ever been able to imagine, or that by the Spirit of God acting in us in such a manner that He causes us to recognize it as such—that we will not avidly receive it nor desire it with all the power of our souls. And this is what the Apostle says, that before he knew our Lord Jesus he persecuted the church of God to the death and ravaged it. He states, *"but when it pleased God to reveal His Son in me ... I did not receive counsel from flesh and blood* (Galatians 1:16); rather, he received the gospel with faith, and notwithstanding all obstacles, advanced His glory with all of His power. Testifying the same of the Jews that if they had truly recognized Jesus, *"they never would have crucified the Lord of glory"* (1 Corinthians 2:8). And that which is the sovereign point of the wisdom of God in this matter—that which also should necessarily accompany the efficacy of His Spirit in our calling and which is inseparable from it—is that He does these things in such a manner that instead of the sorrow which permeates all the actions in which we are seemingly violated, for all constraint seems unpleasant at the time, faith is completely instilled with an unspeakable joy and contentment. For it is impossible either to have known such an excellent truth, or to have tasted such a great love of God towards us, or to see deliverance from such an appalling condemnation, or to see such a glorious hope raised up, or to see in faith the beginning of such an exquisite holiness, each without being completely aroused by them and thus saturated by an inexpressible pleasure and being unable exactly and sufficiently to comprehend such pleasure. In light of this, St. Paul says that this is *"the peace of God which passes all understanding"* (Philippians 4:7), and St. Peter that, believing in Christ we *"rejoice in Him with an unspeakable and glorious joy"* (1 Peter 1:2).

CHAPTER 13

THAT THIS DOCTRINE OF PREDESTINATION DOES NOT LEAD TO SPIRITUAL APATHY NOR EXTINGUISHES CONCERN FOR HOLY LIVING, BUT INVOKES THE OPPOSITE

[163] From what we have deduced here above, it is easy to presume that one must carefully distinguish between the terms "predestination to salvation" and the "predestination to faith,"[1] which are the means and the condition of fulfillment by which we attain them; as much as the predestination to faith is absolute, so to speak, and does not depend upon any condition, the predestination to salvation can only take place according to its effect concerning the presupposition of this prior condition, that man receives it. It is conventional that one would hold the word predestination to refer simply to salvation—as it is commonly held among those who are well informed in the word of God and who do not wish to defer too much to

---

1 Though stated in confusing terms to his reader, Amyraut is attempting to clarify in these two terms "predestination to salvation" (or God's offer and desire of salvation) and "predestination to faith" (the actual accomplishing of salvation/faith), that they should be understood as two distinct actions: (1) Salvation or the offer of salvation as based in man's conditional response to the offer of the gospel and, (2) "Faith" as God's perfect and inviolable election of those who will ultimately be saved. Under the banner of predestination, the term "to salvation" focuses on man's responsibility and necessity of accepting Christ by faith or rejecting that offer of salvation; and the term predestination "to faith" underscores Amyraut's point that God's absolute will in election is predetermined and fixed in eternity past. More clearly, Amyraut's second edition (1658) changes the terminology here significantly where he elucidates that "one must carefully distinguish between God's will (desire) to save men, of which some call against the usage of Scripture, the predestination to salvation, and between the election or predestination of faith." The term predestination to salvation highlights God's desire and intentionality to save mankind, but which is conditional on man's response, whereas God's election of certain men is absolute and unconditional.

the will of man—expecting an indubitable result since it was based upon an absolute decree and did not depend upon any condition. And it seems that even the Apostle Paul employs this meaning when he says that those *"whom God has foreknown, He has predestined them to be conformed to the image of His Son"* (Romans 8:29). For salvation and the conforming to the image of Christ as we have shown above are one and the same thing. And it is clear that the apostle speaks in this place, not of all men equally and generally, but of those whom God *has foreknown*, that is, having foreseen in all ways from His mercy and separated from the others for this inestimable prerogative of faith. But the reason for this is that the "predestination to salvation"[1] being conditional and regarding the whole human race equally[2]—the human race being universally corrupted by sin and incapable of accomplishing the condition upon which salvation depends—it happens necessarily, not by any fault of predestination itself, but by the hardness of the heart and the stubbornness of the human spirit that this first predestination (to salvation) is fruitless for those who have no part in the second, or (election to faith).[3] The term predestination therefore having a certain incommunicable emphasis is customarily and properly reserved for counsels[4] which come to fruition rather than for those in which unbelief and the absence of some prior condition prevent their outcome; for example, Holy Scripture on the one hand does not customarily call those who not having been elected to faith as "predestined" which renders this other predestination (to salvation) useless with respect to itself, while on the other hand Scripture speaks of those who are elected to faith as if they have been absolutely predestined to salvation because of the indubitable result (fulfillment) of the prior condition. And thus it combines, as if there was only a single counsel with respect to them, the conditional predestination to salvation with the absolute election to faith, since in what concerns them, although the one is conditional, it is nevertheless also as certain as if it were absolute because of the infallible and absolute certainty of the fulfillment of the other upon which it depends. And it is for this very reason that the same Scripture which teaches us so dispassionately that Christ

---

1   (1658) edition: "The will of God being conditional ..."
2   (1658) edition: "equally" here omitted.
3   (1658) edition: "... that this first will of God that some call, as I have said, predestination—against the style of Scripture—is fruitless for those who have no part in the second, which is to say in election." *Frustroire* here connotes "fruitless" rather than "frustrated."
4   Counsels as in God's decree to elect.

died universally for all the world, also speaks sometimes in such manner that it seems to indicate that He died only for the small number elected to faith. That is as if He had suffered only for those who taste the fruit of His death and not for those whose own unbelief renders this death frustrated.[1] But because it is necessary to distinguish diligently between those ways of speaking which are born in consideration of the outcomes alone and those resulting from consideration of the covenants themselves, and because we are here treating the counsels of God in all their mystery, it is necessary for us to be on guard against confusing[2] the "predestination to salvation," which depends upon the condition which God requires absolutely of all, with the election to faith, according to which God has ordained to accomplish Himself in order to fulfill this condition in only certain ones.

[166] Against this doctrine thus expounded, no one can charge misrepresentation,[3] which has been customarily charged against the doctrine of predestination, that, if there are some among men predestined to be saved, regardless of what they do (or believe) that they cannot fail to be saved, and, if there are some others eternally reprobate, employ as they will all possible care to obtain salvation, that they are nevertheless excluded from all hope. Were this true, this would produce in the world a horrible confusion and render the preaching of the gospel useless, and extinguish all care for piety and all pursuit of virtue in the souls of men. Is this therefore a question regarding the "predestination to faith?" Certainly none could say "although I believe, I will not, however, be elected to believe." Thus, all those who *do* believe have been previously predestined by the mercy of God to believe, no one being able to believe except by the gift of God as He has declared, and none receiving this gift except by virtue of an eternal election and predestination. Nor could it be said, "Although I will never believe, I will nevertheless be elected and predestined to believe." For all those who have been predestined to believe have (demonstrated) faith. If they never had it, it would be totally absurd to say that they have been predestined to believe. As such, it would be a comparable indulgence to say that someone has been predestined to see, who has nevertheless always kept his eyes shut, or that one has been ordained to live who has never existed and therefore not felt any

---

1 (1658) edition: fruitless.
2 (1658) edition: "confounding this disposition of the will of God which concerns salvation and the …"
3 Calumnie.

movement of life. Certainly Holy Scripture clearly teaches us that there are few of the elect in comparison to others. And experience has always shown this, that the number of those who believe is always very small compared to those who do not believe. Nevertheless, Scripture has neither named nor designated those who are ordained for this. Rather, the Bible offers to us only the love of God who pays regard to all men universally in that He promises them salvation provided that they believe, and the commandment of God which also regards them equally, to receive by faith the Redeemer whom He presents to them. In this manner, none can be exempt from the obligation (requirement) to believe innate in the commandment, for it addresses itself to all; and none should be discouraged as if faith might be useless for him, for the promise of salvation is equally and universally given to all who believe.

[169] Is there, therefore, someone to whom his conscience bears witness that he truly believes? This one has, by faith, the assurance of eternal election. For if only those whom God gives belief have actual saving faith and if He gives it only to those to whom He has decreed from all eternity to give it, the one who believes truly cannot doubt that he has part in the decree[1] of this eternal election. Is there someone who does not believe and who persists in his unbelief to the end? That is truly undeniable evidence that he was not elected to have saving faith, since he did not have nor demonstrate it; yet, this unbelief does not excuse himself before God! For his unbelief does not arise from knowing that he was not ordained to it, but from the hardness of his heart, from the natural hatred that he bears toward God, and because he focuses on the things that are solely pleasing to him. That which he has done has not been out of respect for the secret ordinance of God's election—not struggling for salvation against His will—but by an intolerable contempt for the grace of salvation that God offered to him and through a punishable rebellion against His commandment which taught him and required of him to believe. And truly, the mercy of God toward men concerning His counsels to procure salvation for them consists in two degrees: one which, as it is said, does not go beyond presenting to us the forgiveness of our sins through the Redeemer and takes sovereign pleasure in our salvation providing that through unbelief we do not reject this grace; the other goes so far as to make us believe and prevents salvation from being rejected by us. The first degree is universally manifested to all through the preaching of the gospel,

---

1 Ordinance.

inviting men to faith with the firm and immovable resolution to save them if they believe. Accordingly, the gospel cries through the universe, *Grace, Grace*. The second is not particularly manifested to anyone except by its fulfillment, that is, by the feeling of faith engendered in one's soul. And it has been expressly hidden from humanity whom between them this degree of mercy applies, so that salvation might not be an obstacle to some and a hindrance to the preaching of the gospel for others. Thus, not knowing in particular that one has been ordained to salvation by the counsel of God, no one should presume himself to be reprobate and shut himself off from the hope of salvation, seeing that God is calling him to it. Nor should it be said, "I do not believe because it would be useless for me to do so," since God openly declares that faith will be effective for salvation equally and universally to all those in whom it is found.

[171] More so, truly supposing the case—and this is completely impossible because of the hardness and corruption of man's heart—that there was one of the number of those to whom God has not ordained to give faith who nevertheless truly believed, producing by the power of nature alone that which the others produce through the efficacy of the grace of God in them, that one would be saved without God doing any damage to his decree of eternal predestination. For on the one hand He has ordained not to exclude from salvation any of those who believe, but just the opposite;[1] and on the other hand, although He has predestined some to believe, that is, decreed to give them faith, He has nevertheless not predestined the others not to believe, that is, decreed to prevent them from believing.[2] He is content to leave them in their natural condition and nevertheless to invite them to believe, so that if they have in them some ability to believe they might use

---

1 Emphasizing man's responsibility to believe in Christ within the Reformed doctrine of predestination, fellow French Reformed pastor and defender of Amyraut's views, Jean Daillé, states: "Is it not one of the decrees of God to which we are referred that all those who believe will be saved? For God has decided not only NOT to save any of those who do not believe but also to condemn no one of those who do believe. From this it follows that those who are lost not only could have been saved but would in fact have been saved if they had believed." Letter from Jean Daillé in defense of Amyraut, 1635. Taken from F. P. VanStam, *The Controversy over the Theology of Saumur: 1635–1650*, Ch. 4.

2 Here again Amyraut clearly rejects the traditional Reformed doctrine of supralapsarian double-predestination. Rather, Amyraut contends that though God actively elects some to saving faith, He nevertheless passes over the non-elect, allowing their own depravity, active sin nature, and utter rebellion against God as their deeds of evil to condemn themselves justly.

it. And although He certainly knows and foresees that they will not believe, His foreknowledge however did not cause their unbelief, but rather it is the corruption of their nature. But if this does happen—and this is totally impossible because of the immutable decree of God and His invincible power to execute it—that one of these whom He has predestined to believe did not believe or that one of those who truly believed in accordance with God's election was not saved, then His predestination and the trustworthiness of His promises would be deficient.

[173] Let us then consider this "predestination to salvation." Is it a question of this? Certainly if the doctrine of predestination in this respect is able to cause any damage, it must be either in inducing men not to believe, or in inducing them after having believed to not care about piety and the sanctification of life. But far from it that it is inducing them not to believe, since if they have any knowledge of salvation at all, it induces them necessarily to believe. For if the love that we bear for ourselves and the desire that we naturally have of an eternal happiness attributable to some power above truly exists, since it is impossible to obtain the salvation offered to us without faith, who would then doubt that it is absolutely necessary for him to believe? And, consequently, who would consider faith and unbelief matters of indifference? Certainly, as it has been said, nature has imprinted in man such an ardent desire for his own supreme good, that whatever constitutes it is impossible for him not to follow. Suppose, then, that he knows that this supreme good lies in the salvation of which Christ has authored for us and that it is impossible for him to obtain it except by means of faith, it necessarily follows that his desires carry him toward this salvation and that moreover to attain it, he necessarily will believe. For it is inconceivable how, knowing a supreme good and being persuaded that there is only one way to arrive at it, that he could love and desire this goal and nevertheless view the only means of enjoying it with indifference. Proof of this is seen in those merchants who place their supreme good according to the supposed earthly riches of the Indies; these are not afraid to set out to go there in spite of so many dangers of pirates and shipwrecks. Further, men of war, who consider as their supreme good a victory over their enemies, risk so many perils and do not give any consideration either to death or wounds.

[174] For if this doctrine of predestination does not induce men to disregard faith, it is impossible that it induces them to disregard sanctification, seeing that the one depends necessarily upon the other. And such is the nature of

the gospel, and moreover such is the nature of man, if we consider it as it must be understood, that whoever has truly believed the same also necessarily sanctifies himself and whoever neglects the pursuit of true sanctification, far from actually having true faith, scarcely has a shadow of it in him. And it is this which is stated so expressly by St. John where he states, *"who is in the light loves his brother, and whoever does not love his brother and says that he is in the light is a liar and the truth is not in him. Indeed, whoever hates his brother is in the darkness and walks in darkness and does not know where it is he is going, because the darkness has blinded his eyes"* (1 John 2:9–11). Thus, it is not possible that these two things are divided equally, a true knowledge of Christ the Savior and Redeemer which consists in faith, and the absence of the charity in which lies the sanctification of man.

[175]   There is more. We have said that salvation consists in the reparation of the image of God in us and that this divine restitution lies in two respects, holiness and happiness; moreover, that this holiness is the first and more excellent part. It would therefore be madness to say, "If I am predestined, I will be saved, regardless how I conduct my of life." For this is as if someone said, "If I am predestined to be white, I will be white even though I am black, and that I blacken myself perpetually." Similarly, if one said "If I am predestined to be a good man, I will be a good man even though I remain an evil man" or such as "If I am predestined to live, I will live, regardless of whether I remain forever lying and rotting in the tomb;" or last, "If I am elect unto salvation, I will be saved even though I willingly damn myself." Such is the discourse not of a man in his right mind, but of a madman.

[176]   For since the predestination to salvation[1] is principally predestination to holiness, how could we wish that God should lead us to the end to which we are destined, except by sanctifying us? And how will He sanctify us without illuminating our minds or reforming our will? And how could the illumination of the mind and the reformation of the will survive with a determined resolution to love the darkness and the works of darkness? In fact, if our reasonable faculties are so naturally composed that they are capable of being touched by the admiration and the love of beautiful, excellent things and knowing that the possession of these qualities constitutes their perfection and their goal—since we are called to be clothed again in the new man

---

1   (1658) edition: "For since the counsel of God which concerns salvation principally concerns holiness ..."

created according to God in justice and true holiness, that is, to bear the image of God Himself in those qualities which are the most beautiful and most glorious of His nature—who will be so coarse as to think that he is able to attain this goal by turning his back and giving himself to that which we are directly opposed? All things incline naturally to their proper ends. For example, heavy objects sink and are destined by nature to occupy the center of the earth. This is their resting ground, the place which has been ordained for them for the preservation of their being. And they bear a predisposition so strong to it that it is impossible to turn them away from it. Given therefore that a heavy object, such as the earth, has some knowledge of its own nature and its own end, that is, of the end to which the universal laws of the world call it, do you think that to come to the center of the universe it would try on the contrary to elevate itself and that it would imagine that in this way it could arrive at the resting ground ordained for it by nature? If therefore the wisdom of the One who has directed all things in the world to their ends has been such that by the means of the instincts which He has given them they move themselves from there even without intelligence, how much more will man, who has been given a knowledge of his own, move himself there by the desires and the affections which excite in him this light of wisdom which has been communicated to him through the grace of the gospel.

[178] As for that part of the image of God which consists in happiness, seeing that it is so attached to the other and so depends upon it that they are entirely inseparable, who will promise himself that he can disjoin them and so possess the latter separately after having trampled under foot the former and more excellent? Or who will not judge that whoever neglects the one shuts himself off from the hope of the latter and consequently that he must join them together, indeed almost only esteeming happiness as merely the splendor, if it must be said thus, of the piety and the holiness which precede it? But the fact that the doctrine of predestination is attacked with these reproaches demonstrates that the great percentage of the world deceives itself in the thoughts which it has about the nature of salvation. For since the fall of man, we love ourselves out of an extreme nature and we love God extremely little; indeed, we even hate Him and the things which are pleasing to Him, and when someone speaks to us of salvation, we immediately imagine our own contentment and ease. As for that which concerns holiness, either we do not consider it at all or, if we think of it, we do so only to make it serve for the acquisition of the other things. In this way, if God has broken the

link which binds them together, we will entirely despise holiness and only wish to be saved in order to be made comfortable. Thus, are we by nature mercenaries and slaves, only loving piety and virtue for the recompense which we promise ourselves follows it, and not pursuing vice because of the deprivation of well-being and the feeling of pain which accompanies it? And would we not be very pleased if, even by fulfilling our more carnal lusts, we could also obtain eternal happiness which we crave? Such that while we may bear the name of Christians, most of us, however, in this respect are like Muslims and do not imagine any other paradise than one that is delightful and sensual,[1] not such as it ought to really be, holy, pure and chaste. Whereas those who are truly saturated with faith in our Lord Jesus and are touched by the excellence of the gospel consider these things from an altogether different perspective and feel at least as much obligated to love God for redemption from the power of sin through sanctification as for the redemption from the condemnation of it by the forgiveness of the offense, as much for having been delivered from that which merits death as for having been retrieved from death itself; as much for the beginning of true holiness in them as for the down payment of the possessions of His heritage; and as much for the hope of being someday like Him in purity, when they will see Him as He is, as for the assurance of being conformed to Him in glory. And nevertheless joining these two things together and considering in them together the immense love that God has displayed toward them, they are enraptured in admiration and profoundly stirred by emotion and by gratitude for such an incomprehensible mercy. That is, if we are truly Christians, this is the most lively and most efficacious motive for piety and virtue and the one which best represents the condition of the blessed spirits which are in heaven and the condition of which we will be when after the resurrection of the body God has received us in glory. For then we will not love God either through the fear of pain or cursing, knowing as much that we will there be beyond danger, or for the hope of happiness, since we will there be full of joy, but because God is supremely worthy of love because of His virtues, notably His goodness, and because, not content to testify of His goodness toward us, He has displayed an immense mercy in sending His only Son to the world to redeem us from sin and death and in overcoming by the efficacy of His grace in us, according to the intent decreed in His election,

---

1 Voluptueux.

our natural unbelief, so that this redemption might not be unfruitful for us. And this is that which St. Paul calls, *"To contemplate as in a mirror the glory of the Lord with an unveiled face, and to be transformed into the very image from glory to glory, as by the Spirit of the Lord"* (2 Corinthians 3:18).[1]

---

1 In the original text, the verse is erroneously misquoted as 2 Corinthians 2:18.

CHAPTER 14

HOW THE DOCTRINE OF PREDESTINATION FILLS THE CONSCIENCE OF THE FAITHFUL WITH JOY AND CONSOLATION

[182] It is difficult to express the comfort with which this doctrine fills those who have felt the efficacy of the grace of God and of the preaching of the gospel of Christ, which manifests itself as much in the faith with which they have embraced it as the beginnings of true sanctification which is engendered in their souls. For do these have to search for the assurance of their predestination, and by consequence, the testimonies of this second degree of the merciful love of God toward men of which we have spoken above?[1] They do not have to climb into heaven in order to see if their names are written there, nor ask God to open His books[2] for them. But, as someone who wants to know if God has ordained that he would someday be alive on this earth, he should consider for himself the movement of his own pulse, the pattern of his body, the functions of his senses, the desires of his affections, the anxieties of his mind, and should gather from these undeniable marks of life within him, reasoning that, since all these things are in me, I live. And since I live, it must have been ordained that I am alive and living the life similar to all men appearing in the world according to the counsel of God and not by chance. Thus the believer, wanting to be assured of his election to the spiritual life in Christ, will feel, if one can speak this way, the pulse of his soul, and recognizing in his understanding an extraordinary illumination, in his conscience a profound peace through the assurance of forgiveness, and in his will (and in all his emotions), a passionate love toward the One who

---

1 Concerning the benefit of sanctification for those who are elect and who are being conformed daily into the image of Christ.
2 *Registres*.

is the Author of this peace and toward similar men; he will also feel all that concerns true life and a profound hope of another life than this terrestrial one, finding by faith, I say, all these same marks in the life of Christ, and will reason that since he could only have these things by the grace of God, as Scripture teaches, and that since this grace is only communicated[1] by virtue of this election, it must necessarily be that he has a part in it and that God has loved him before the foundation of the world. For there is no one who would not easily judge what great consolation this consideration is capable of giving a good soul.

[184] Can one find some contentment in seeing his formerly miserable condition changed into an excellent state? We were by nature slaves to sin which absolutely reigned in us and, by sin, slaves of Satan who labors with efficacy in the children of rebellion, subjects of the kingdom of darkness and were covered in sin from birth; we were children of evil in imitation and resemblance of his wickedness; we were dead in our trespasses and sins, and so it can be said again, we were the most miserable of things. However, by faith in our Lord Jesus we are set free, delivered from chains and from the dominion of Satan, having been transported to the kingdom of the marvelous light of God, adopted to be among the number of His children, partakers of His nature, raised from the dead, and given to the joy of true life which lies in holiness and justice. Such is the joy of slaves who have seen themselves set free, of captives who have seen themselves loosed from their bonds and chains, of the dead who have arisen from the grave and consider the corruption which they have been spared, and of those who have been fostered in dark prisons when they finally see a marvelously sweet and pleasant light. Such would be even the joy of a wretched demon, if he were to see himself softened and converted into an angel, just as would be the consolation of the faithful one when he compares himself with and considers the condition from which he escaped with the one to which he enters. Indeed, so much more are the excellent of things the greater the former corruption, and how much more exquisite, beautiful, and intelligent man's nature is when it is covered by the virtues which constitute the perfection of his being, while equally so much more the ugly and the more horrible it becomes when he degenerates and lapses into a contrary condition.

[186] Now, is the hope of some great good able to give us true contentment?

---

1 Given or rendered.

Faith is necessarily accompanied by the hope of deliverance from evils that we deserve, and of pleasure of the good things that Christ has acquired for us, of which these exceed all human imagination and comprehension. Because neither tortures, nor hells, nor crosses, nor gallows, nor racks, nor fires, nor the most extreme horrors equal that which we deserve and which awaits us in hell. The image themselves of flaming lakes of fire and sulfur are only employed to represent such horrors to us, because they are alternately all that can be said and shown to our minds of that which is most horrible and frightful. Neither the most delicious banquets, nor the most vigorous well-being, nor the greatest treasures, nor the most noteworthy and magnificent glories, nor the most brilliant admirations[1] of this earth equal that which Christ has acquired for us. The very crowns of kings and the glory of empires are only employed to describe such greatness to us because they are alternately the things which customarily incite the greatest admiration or excite the greater lusts of men. Accordingly, the Apostle, in comparing the happiness that the gospel has brought to us in filling the present again with the knowledge of Christ with what the Patriarchs had seen in the Old Testament, has said that according to the words of the prophet, "*these are things that eye had not seen, nor ear had heard, nor which had not entered into the heart of man, that God has prepared for those who love Him and which He has revealed by His Sprit*"(1 Corinthians 2:9). We can say this in even stronger terms by comparing the glory of heaven to which we aspire to the state of this present earth, in order to illuminate that which is the knowledge of Christ through the gospel.

[188] Finally, can we draw some consolation from the certain and undeniable assurance that we will never degenerate from this state of holiness to which it has pleased God to begin in us by giving us saving faith in Jesus Christ, but that we will persevere in it until the end, and even so far as to attain to perfection in the heavenly places. So that, I say, we will never fall again into the peril of death and the curse from which we have been pulled, but will certainly gain true life and eternal glory. We have this assurance in this doctrine and without it our consolation would be completely defective. Since faith does not come from ourselves but is a gift of God, and since this gift proceeds itself from His free will without having had regard either for our works or the dispositions and preparations of our spirits, or to some condition

---

1   *Dignités.*

that He foresaw should be in our persons, why would He change the decree which has no other cause than His own will, being constant and immutable in all other things? Our eternal salvation depends on this condition which we call faith; this faith then depends upon the grace of God in us and upon the power of His Spirit; further, this grace and this power of the Spirit depend upon therefore the counsel of election within God, and this counsel, having no other foundation than His will, is constant and irrevocable. From this, it necessarily follows that the outcome of all this and the joy of our salvation is at every point beyond doubt.

[189] Why then, do I say, that this depends upon a counsel which has no other cause than His free will? Certainly this is true when we compare ourselves with those to whom He has not given the same grace and then seek for the reason why, being all in the same condition, and yet He has nevertheless preferred us to them. There is no other reason for this other than that it has thus pleased Him to do so, "*to have mercy toward him to whom He has mercy, and to have compassion toward him to who He has compassion.*"[1] But this is nevertheless a stroke of particular favor which He has shown to us, a special degree of love with which it has pleased Him to honor us, His good pleasure having been to foreknow us in this manner, which is to say to anticipate within us of His love and to overtake us in His mercy. For if He has loved us before we had faith to the degree that He wished to give it to us, will He not love us enough to preserve it after having given it to us? If He has so loved us from the time we were yet His enemies, how could He not love us more now that we are His friends? If His mercy has been such toward us while we were children of evil, will His compassions diminish when we are His children and when He has begun to restore in us the beauty of His image? If after having decreed to send His Son into the world to redeem the human race He ordained to give us faith and by this faith to give us to His Son, so that this redemption might not be useless, will He not love us now to the extent that having begun to be true participants in this redemption we might not return to the former curse? And is this not so much more true since the condition of those who fall back in that way is much worse and more unhappy than that of those who never left it? If finally He has so loved us while we were yet of the world, and consequently while His Son did not pray for us, being content to present Himself to the world outwardly as Savior,

---

1   Romans 9:15.

and furthermore while He did not interpose the efficacy of His intercession on our behalf—for those who do not believe are of the world and He says expressly that *"He does not pray for the world"* (John 17:9)—now that we are no longer of the world and that we are in Christ, and now that as He had resolved in His eternal counsel, God has truly and in fact given us to Him so as to enter into Him by faith and be made of the one and same vine, how could He not render indissoluble this holy communion and have regard for the prayers of His only Son?' Christ prays, *"Now I am no longer in the world, but they are in the world and I am coming to you. Holy Father, keep them in your name, the very ones that you have given to me, so that they may be one, even as we are. I do not ask you to take them out of the world, but that you might keep them from the evil one. They are not of the world, even as I am not of the world. Sanctify them through the truth. For your word is truth. Now I do not pray to you for them alone, but also for those who will believe in me through their word, so that all might be one, as you, Father, are in me and I in you, that they also might be one in us."*[1]

[192] Thus, this second degree of the love of God upon which His election depends produces a third as tender and intense, as constant and as invariable as the other.[2] It is this which He carries for us when He sees that by His grace we are beginning to bear the characteristics of His image. According to this second degree, He *"has loved us so as to adopt us in Christ"*[3] and to make us His children. According to the third, He loves us in that having truly and in fact been adopted, we are already His children and participants in the holiness of His nature. According to the second degree, He has loved us so that we might love Him. According to the third, He loves us because we love Him in return. According to the second degree, He loves us in order to begin in us the work of our salvation. According to the third, He loves us because it has already begun and because He wishes to perfect it in us. And it is in light of this fact that the Holy Scriptures, particularly the Apostle Paul among the

---

1   John 17:11, 15–17, 20–21.

2   At times and somewhat confusingly, Amyraut intersperses his metaphors and illustrations. Where he speaks here of the degrees of love and counsels, Amyraut is generically referencing three phases within conversion: the first degree is the outward faith which man shows to God in conversion and which is conditional by nature. The second degree is God's absolute counsel based upon His unconditional love whereby He elects men to salvation. The third degree is the reciprocal love demonstrated in sanctification whereby the elect pursue holiness in Christ's image and God renders more sanctification by His Spirit which produces in us fruitfulness and assurance of faith.

3   Ephesians 1:4–5.

other holy writers, considering how great are the mercies of God toward the elect and fashioning for this consideration reasons for their consultation through the assurances of their perseverance in this grace, Paul speaks of the sending of God's Son into the world as if it has been ordained only for them and as if other men do not have a part in the propitiation that He has made for sins, although as we have seen above, He has been sent to save all men equally,[1] provided that through unbelief they do not show themselves unworthy of the mercy which is offered[2] to them. For if you compare the love that God has shown to men in this covenant with the price of the one He carried and that He extends to the elect, the first of which the effect depends upon the execution of the condition which He requires of them is negligible,[3] although it might be marvelously great when considered precisely and absolutely in itself. And, if you contemplate the fruit which results from the propitiation made by Christ, the unbelief of some preventing that they can receive anything makes it seem by comparison that He has only had regard for those in whom He has ordained to make it fruitful. Therefore, we will finish this small treatise with the memorable words of that excellent Apostle: "*We also glory in our sufferings, because we know that suffering produces perseverance; perseverance, character; and character, hope. And hope does not put us to shame, because God's love has been poured out into our hearts through the Holy Spirit, who has been given to us. You see, at just the right time, when we were still powerless, Christ died for the ungodly. Very rarely will anyone die for a righteous person, though for a good person someone might possibly dare to die. But God demonstrates His own love for us in this: While we were still sinners, Christ died for us. Since we have now been justified by His blood, how much more shall we be saved from God's wrath through Him! For if, while we were God's enemies, we were reconciled to Him through the death of his Son, how much more, having been reconciled, shall we be saved through His life*" (Romans 5:3–11). And elsewhere: "*What, then, shall we say in response to these things? If God is for us, who can be against us? He who did not spare his own Son, but gave him up for us all—how will he not also, along with him, graciously give us all things? Who will bring any charge against those whom God has chosen? It is God who justifies. Who then is the one who condemns? No one. Christ Jesus who died—more than that, who was raised to life—is at the right*

---

1 (1658) edition: "equally" is again omitted here.
2 Presentée.
3 "… *n'est quasi pas considerable…*" lit. "is not half or partially considerable."

hand of God and is also interceding for us. Who shall separate us from the love of Christ? Shall trouble or hardship or persecution or famine or nakedness or danger or sword? In all these things we are more than conquerors through him who loved us. For I am convinced that neither death nor life, neither angels nor demons, neither the present nor the future, nor any powers, neither height nor depth, nor anything else in all creation, will be able to separate us from the love of God that is in Christ Jesus our Lord" (Romans 8:28–39). To Him be all glory forever and ever, Amen.

THE END.

APPENDIX[1]

THE

Acts, Canons, Decisions, and Decrees

OF THE

Twenty seventh Synod

OF

The Reformed Churches

OF

FRANCE,

Assembled under His Majesty's Authority and Permission

AT

ALENÇON

IN THE

PROVINCE of *NORMANDY*

on Wednesday the twenty-seventh of May, and ended Thursday the ninth of *July*.

In the Year of our Lord God, 1637.

Being the twenty-eighth year of the Reign of

LOUIS XIII

King of *FRANCE* and *NAVARRE*

---

[1] Alan C. Clifford, Edited extracts from John Quick, *Synodicon in Gallia Reformata* (London: 1692), ii. 352–57.

THE
Acts, Canons, Decisions, and Decrees,
OF THE
Twenty seventh Synod
OF
The Reformed Churches
OF
FRANCE,
Assembled under his Majesty's Authority and Permission,
AT
ALANSON,
IN THE
PROVINCE of NORMANDY,

On Wednesday the twenty seventh of *May*, and ended Thursday the ninth of *July*.

In the Year of our Lord God, 1637.

Being the twenty eighth Year of the Reign of

LOUIS XIII.
King of *FRANCE* and *NAVARRE.*

AMYRAUT AT ALENÇON

The Determination and Decision of that Affair concerning the doctrine and writings of the Sieurs Amyraut and Testard, Pastors, and Professor of Divinity in the Academy of Saumur.

12. The Sieurs Testard Pastor of the Church of Blois, and Amyraut Pastor and Professor of Theology in the Church and Academy of Saumur, came in person unto this Synod, and declared, that they understood from common fame, how that both at home and abroad, and by the consultations and proceedings of sundry Provinces, as also from divers books written against them and their printed labours, they were blamed for that doctrine which they had published to the world;[1] that therefore at the first opening of the Synod they presented themselves before it, not knowing but that their cause might be debated whenas the Confession of Faith came to be read, and that they appeared to give an account of it, and such explanations of their doctrine, as the most reverend Synod should judge needful; and to submit themselves unto its judgement, and consequently to demand its protection for the support of their innocence, hoping that this favour would not be denied them; because they were fully persuaded in their consciences, that they had never taught, either by word or writing, any doctrine repugnant to the Word of God, to our Confession of Faith, Catechism, Liturgy, or Canons of the National Synods of Alès and Charenton, which had ratified those of Dort, and which they had signed with their hands, and were ready to seal even with their heart-blood.

13. And the Sieur de la Place, Pastor and Professor in the Church and

---

[1] viz. Paul Testard, Eirenikon, *seu Synopsis doctrinae de natura et gratia* (Blaesii, 1633); Moïse Amyraut, *Brief Traitte de la Predestination* (Saumur, 1634); *Eschantillon de la doctrine de Calvin, touchant le predestination* (Saumur, 1636). This 75-page preface to *Six Sermons* included numerous examples of Calvin's statements. Amyraut thus demonstrated that 'his doctrine was a faithful reproduction of Calvin's theology' (Armstrong, 83).

Academy of Saumur, reported also from the said Academy, that he was charged by it to render an account of the grounds and reasons which induced him to approve and license the works and writings of Monsieur Amyraut, which he did, according to the privilege granted by the Discipline unto our Academies. Moreover, the Sieur Ouzan, Elder in the Church of Saumur, being admitted into the Synod, declared, that the said Church understanding that Monsieur Amyraut, one of its pastors, was brought into trouble for his doctrine, though both by it, and his most exemplary and godly conversation, they had been always exceedingly edified, had given him an express charge to testify unto it before this grave Assembly, and most humbly to commend unto their Reverences the innocency and honour of his ministry.

14. There were also tendered unto the Lord Commissioner the letters, but not opened, which were sent unto the Synod from the Churches and Academies of Geneva and Leyden, and from the Sieurs du Moulin Pastor and Professor in Theology at Sedan, and Rivet Pastor and Professor at Leyden, together with the Treatises composed by them, and he collated copies of the Approbations given by the Doctors in the Faculty of Theology at Leyden, Franeker and Groningen, unto the Treatise of the said Professor Rivet: which letters being opened by the Lord Commissioner, and their contents perused by him, he allowed the reading of them unto the Assembly. The Assembly did likewise read the letters writ by Monsieur Vignier Pastor in the Church of Blois, and by Monsieur le Faucheur Pastor in the Church of Paris, in which they offer their sentiments for reconciling the controversies arisen about the writings of the said Testard and Amyraut, and their opponents.

15. Moreover, the apologetical letters of the Sieurs Vignier and Garnier, Pastors of the Churches of Blois and Marchenoir, were read, who informed the Synod, that by virtue of a Commission given them by the Province of Berry to examine the theological writings which might be composed either by the Pastors or others of their Province, they had given their attestation and approbation to the book of the said Monsieur Testard, and had given an account of this their judgement unto the Provincial Synod assembled in the year 1634; and the extracts of those their writings were produced.

16. Those papers having been all read, and the aforesaid Sieurs Testard and Amyraut having been divers times heard, and the Assembly having in a very long debate considered the difficulties of those questions raised by them, did constitute the Sieurs Commarc Pastor in the Church of Verteuil, Charles Pastor in the Church of Montauban, de L'Angle Pastor in the Church of

Rouen, Petit Pastor and Professor in the Church and Academy of Nîmes, le Blanc Pastor and Professor in the Academy of Die, de Bons Pastor in the Church of Chalons upon Saône, and Daillé Pastor in the Church of Paris, a Committee a digest and reduce into order the explications which had been given, or might hereafter be given by the before-mentioned Testard and Amyraut, and that they should accordingly as soon as it was finished bring in their report.

17. And the said Committee having discharged their trust, and made their report unto the Synod, the before-mentioned M. Testard and Amyraut were again introduced, and did with the deepest seriousness protest before God, that it was never in their thoughts to propound or teach any doctrine whatever, but what was agreeable to the known and common expositions of our Creed, and contained in our Confession of Faith, and in the Decisions of the National Synod held at Charenton, in the year 1623; all which they were ready to sign with their best blood.

18. And pursuant hereunto, explaining their opinion about the universality of Christ's death, they declared, That Jesus Christ died for all men sufficiently, but for the elect only effectually: and that consequentially his intention was to die for all men in respect of the sufficiency of his satisfaction, but for the elect only in respect of its quickening and saving virtue and efficacy; which is to say, that Christ's will was that the sacrifice of his cross should be of an infinite price and value, and most abundantly sufficient to expiate the sins of the whole world; yet nevertheless the efficacy of his death appertains only unto the elect; so that those who are called by the preaching of the Gospel, to participate by faith in the effects and fruits of his death, being invited seriously, and God vouchsafing them all external means needful for their coming to Him, and showing them in good earnest, and with the greatest sincerity by His Word, what would be well-pleasing to Him, if they should not believe in the Lord Jesus Christ, but perish in their obstinacy and unbelief; this cometh not from any defect of virtue or sufficiency in the sacrifice of Jesus Christ, nor yet for want of summons or serious invitations unto faith or repentance, but only from their own fault. And as for those who do receive the doctrine of the Gospel with the obedience of faith, they are according to the irrevocable promise of God, made partakers of the effectual virtue and fruit of Christ Jesus's death; for this was the most free counsel and gracious purpose both of God the Father, in giving his Son for the salvation of mankind, and of the Lord Jesus Christ, in suffering the pains of death, that the efficacy

thereof should particularly belong unto all the elect, and to them only, to give them justifying faith, and by it to bring them infallibly unto salvation, and thus effectually to redeem all those and none other, who were from all eternity from among all people, nations and tongues, chosen unto salvation. Whereupon, although the Assembly were well satisfied, yet nevertheless they decreed, that for the future, that phrase of Jesus Christ's dying equally for all, should be forborne, because that term equally was formerly, and might be so again, an occasion of stumbling unto many.

19. And as for the conditional decree, of which mention is made in the aforesaid Treatise of Predestination, the said Sieurs Testard and Amyraut declared, that they do not, nor ever did understand any other thing, than God's will revealed in His Word, to give grace and life unto believers; and that they called this in none other sense a conditional will than that of an *anthropopeia*, because God promiseth not the effects thereof, but upon condition of faith and repentance. And they added farther, that although the propositions resulting from the manifestation of this will be conditional, and conceived under an *if*, or *it may be*; as, if thou believest thou shalt be saved; if a man repent of his sins, they shall be forgiven him; yet nevertheless this doth not suppose in God an ignorance of the event, nor an impotency as to the execution, nor any inconstancy as to His will, which is always firmly accomplished, and ever unchangeable in itself, according to the nature of God, in which there is no variableness nor shadow of turning.

20. And the said Sieur Amyraut did particularly protest, as he had formerly published unto the world, that he never gave the name of universal or conditional predestination unto this will of God than by way of concession, and accommodating it unto the language of the adversary: Yet forasmuch as many are offended at this expression of his, he offered freely to raze it out of those places, wherever it did occur, promising also to abstain from it for the future: and both he and the Sieur Testard acknowledged, that to speak truly and accurately according to the usage of sacred Scripture, there is none other Decree of Predestination of men unto eternal life and salvation, than the unchangeable purpose of God, by which according to the most free and good pleasure of His will, He hath out of mere grace chosen in Jesus Christ unto salvation before the foundation of the world, a certain number of men in themselves neither better nor more worthy than others, and that He hath decreed to give them unto Jesus Christ to be saved, and that He would call and draw them effectually to communion with Him by His Word

and Spirit. And they did, in consequence of this holy doctrine, reject their error, who held that faith, and the obedience of faith, holiness, godliness and perseverance, are not the fruits and effects of this unchangeable decree unto glory, but conditions or causes, without which election could not be passed; which conditions or causes are antecedently requisite, and foreseen as if they were already accomplished in those who were fit to be elected, contrary to what is taught us by the sacred Scripture, Acts 13:48 and elsewhere.

21. And whereas they have made distinct decrees in this counsel of God, the first of which is to save all men through Jesus Christ, if they shall believe in him; the second to give faith unto some particular persons: they declared, that they did this upon none other account, than of accommodating it unto that manner and order which the spirit of man observeth in his reasonings for the succour of his own infirmity; they otherwise believing, that though they considered this decree as diverse, yet it was formed in God in one and the self same moment, without any succession of thought, or order of priority and posteriority. The will of this most supreme and incomprehensible Lord, being but one only eternal act in him; so that could we but conceive of things as they be in him from all eternity, we should comprehend these decrees of God by one only act of our understanding, as in truth they be but one only act of his eternal and unchangeable will.

22. The Synod having heard these declarations from the Sieurs Testard and Amyraut, it enjoined them and all others to refrain from those terms of conditional, frustratory, or revocable Decree; and that they should rather choose the word *Will*, whereby to express that sentiment of theirs, and by which they would signify the revealed Will of God, commonly called by divines *voluntas* signe.

23. And whereas in sundry places marked in the writings of the before-mentioned Monsieur Testard and Amyraut, they have ascribed unto God, as it were, a notion of velleity, and strong affections, and vehement desires of things which He hath not, nor will ever effectuate; they having declared, that by those figurative ways of speaking, and anthropopathetical, they designed, to speak properly, none other thing than this, that if men were obedient to the commandments and invitations of God, their faith and obedience would be most acceptable unto Him, according as was before expressed by them. The Assembly hearing this their explication, did enjoin them to use such expressions as these, with that sobriety and prudence, that they might

not give the least occasion of offence unto any person, nor cause them to conceive of God in any way unsuitable to His glorious nature.

24. Monsieur Testard and Amyraut declared farther, that although the doctrines obvious to us in the works of creation and providence, do teach and preach repentance, and invite us to seek the Lord, who would be found of us; yet nevertheless, by reason of the horrible blindness of our nature, and its universal corruption, no man was ever this way converted; yea, and it is utterly impossible that any one should be converted but by hearing of the Word of God, which is the seed of our regeneration, and the instrument of the Holy Ghost, whose efficacy and virtue only is able to illuminate our understandings, and to change the hearts and affections of the children of men.

25. And forasmuch as the Word of God hath always revealed the knowledge of the Lord our Redeemer, the said Sieurs did farther protest, that no one man was ever, nor can be saved, without some certain measure of this knowledge, less indeed under the Old Testament, but greater under the New, the death and resurrection of the Son of God being most plainly and distinctly manifested in the Gospel; and they hold it as an undoubted truth, that now under the New Covenant, the distinct knowledge of Christ is absolutely necessary for all persons who are come to years of discretion in order to their obtaining of eternal salvation: And they do from their very heart anathematize all those who believe or teach that man may be saved any other way than by the Merit of our Lord Jesus Christ, or in any religion besides the Christian.

26. And whereas divers persons were much offended at the Professor Amyraut for calling that knowledge of God, which men might gain from the consideration of His works and providence (unless their corruption were extreme) by the name of faith: The said Professor declared, that he did it, because he reckoned that that persuasion which some have, that there is a God, and that He is a rewarder, may bear that name; he owning however that St Paul did simply and plainly stile it the knowledge of God, 1 Cor. 1:21. The Assembly enjoined him not to give the name of faith to any other knowledge of God, but unto that which is engendered in us by the Holy Ghost, and by the preaching of His Word, according as the Scripture useth it, whether thereby to point out unto us the faith of God's ancient saints, or this which is now under the New Testament, and necessarily accompanied with a distinct knowledge of Christ.

27. And as for man's natural impotency, either to believe, or to desire and

do the things that belong unto salvation; both the said Sieurs Amyraut and Testard protested, that man had none other power than that of the Holy Spirit of God, which is only able to heal him, by an interior illuminating of his understanding, and bending of his will by that gracious, invincible and ineffable operation, which He only exerts upon the hearts of those vessels of Grace which are elect of God.

28. They did farther declare, that this impotency was in us from our birth, for which cause it may be called natural; and they have called it physical or natural, nor ever did refuse so doing, unless when they would signify that it is voluntary, and conjoined with malice and obstinacy; when as man despiseth and rejecteth the invitations of God, which he would receive and embrace, provided his heart were well and fittingly disposed within itself.

29. And Monsieur Testard added particularly, that this doth not in the least derogate from what he had asserted concerning two callings, the one real, and other verbal, given by God unto men, whereby they may be saved if they will, [since] that he intended thereby to signify nothing else, but that their impotency to convert themselves was not of the same kind with that of a man, who having lost his eyes or legs, was willing with all his heart to see and walk, but that this impotency sprung from the malice of the heart itself. The Assembly having heard him thus express himself, enjoined him to abstain from these terms, and not to use them unless with very much prudence and discretion, and to join with them such needful glosses and explications, as thereby it may appear, that man is so depraved by nature, that he cannot of himself will any good without the special Grace of God, which may produce in us by His Holy Spirit both to will and to do according to His good pleasure.

30. And those afore-mentioned minister and professor, Testard and Amyraut, having acquiesced in all, as above declared, and having sworn and subscribed to it, the Assembly gave them the right hand of fellowship by the hand of the Moderator, and they were honourably dismissed to the exercise of their respective charges.

BIBLIOGRAPHY

PRIMARY SOURCES

Amyraut, Moïse. *Brief Traitté de la Prédestination et Ses Principales Dépendances.* (Saumur: Lesnier & Desbordes, 1634).

_____. *Brief Traité de la Prédestination: Avec l'Eschantillon de la Doctrine de Calvin sur le Mesme sujet; et La Response a M. de la Grace et Autres Questions de Theologie.* (Saumur: Isaac Desbordes, 1658).

_____. *Defense de la Doctrine de Calvin Sur le Sujet de l'Election and Réprobation.* (Saumur: Isaac Desbordes, 1644).

_____. *Dissertationes Theologicae.* 6 vols. (Saumur: Desbordes, 1645).

_____. *L'Eschantillon de la Doctrine de Calvin Touchant la Predestination.* (Saumur: Desbordes, 1658).

_____. *Sermons sur Divers Textes de la Sainte Écriture: Prononcés en Divers Lieux.* (Saumur: Isaac Desbordes, 1653).

_____. *Six Sermons de la Nature, Estendue, Necessité, Dispensation, et Efficace de l'Evangile.* (Saumur: Claude Girard & Daniel de Lerpiniere, 1636).

Amyraut, Moïse, Louis Cappel, and Josué La Place. *Syntagma Thesium Theologicarum in Academia Salmuriensi Variis Temporibus Disputatarum*, Editio Secunda, 4 parts. (Saumur: Joannes Lesner, 1664).

Baxter, Richard. *Universal Redemption of Mankind by the Lord Jesus Christ.* (London: Printed for John Salsbury at the Rising Sun in Cornhill, 1694). Reset edition available at www.quintapress.com/PDF_Books.html.

Beza, Theodore. *A Briefe and Pithie Some of the Christian Faith Made in Forme of a Confession, with a Confutation of all Such Superstitious Errours, as Are Contrary Thereunto.* Translated by Robert Fills. (London, NP, 1563).

_____. *Ad Acta Colloquii Montisbelgardensis Tubingae Edita Theodori Bezae Responsio Pars Altera.* (Geneva, 1588).

_____. *A Booke of Christian Questions and Answers: Wherein are Set Forth* the *Chief Points of the Christian Religion*. Translated by Arthur Golding. (London: W. How, 1574).

_____. *Cours sur Les Epîtres aux Romains et aux Hebrieux 1564–66: d'Après Les Notes de Marcus Widler*. Eds. P. Fraenkel and L. Perrotet. (Geneva, NP, 1988).

_____. *Novum Testamentum*, 1560 edition. (New York: D. Appleton, 1861).

_____. *Propositions and Principles of Divinity*. Translated by Antoine de la Faye. (Edinburgh: Waldegraue, 1585).

_____. *Quaestionum et Responsionum Christianarum Pars Altera: Quae Est de Sacramentis*. (Geneva, 1576).

_____. *Tractiones Theologicae*, 3 vols. (Geneva, 1570–1582).

Calvin, John. *Calvin's Commentaries*, 21 vols. Translated by W. Pringle. (Grand Rapids: Baker, 2009).

_____. *Concerning the Eternal Predestination of God*. Translated by J.K.S. Reid. (London, 1961).

_____. *Institutes of the Christian Religion*. Edited by John T. McNeill. Translated by Ford Lewis Battles. 2 vols. The Library of Christian Classics 20–21. Philadelphia: Westminster, 1960. *Institutio Christianae Religionis*. Vols. 3–5 of *Joannis Calvini opera selecta*. Edited by P. Barth and G. Niesel. 5 vols. (Munich: Kaiser, 1926–36).

_____. *Sermons on Isaiah's Prophecy of the Death and Passion of Christ*. Translated by T.H.L. Parker. (London: James Clarke & Co, 2002).

Cotgrave, Randale. *A Dictionarie of the French and English Tongues*. (London: Adam Islip, 1611).

Davenant, John, "Dissertation on the Death of Christ" in *An Exposition of the Epistle of St. Paul to the Colossians*. (London: Hamilton, Adams and Co., 1833). Reset edition reprinted as Davenant, John, *Dissertation on the Death of Christ* (Weston Rhyn: Quinta Press, 2006)

Kimedoncius, Jacob, *The Redemption of Mankind: Three Books: Wherein the Controversy of the Universality of the Redemption and Grace by Christ, and his Death for All Men, is Largely Handled*, trans., by Hugh Ince. (London: Imprinted by Felix Kingston, 1598).

Owen, John. *The Death of Death in the Death of Christ* (1684), rev. ed. (Carlisle, PA: Banner of Truth Trust, 2013).

Quick, John. *Synodicon in Gallia Reformata*. Two volumes. (London: Parkhurst and Robinson, 1692).

Turretin, Francis. *Institutes of Elenctic Theology*. Three volumes. Translated by George Musgrave Giger. (Phillipsburg, NJ: P & R Publishing, 1992–1994).
Ursinus, Zacharias. *The Commentary of Dr. Zacharias Ursinus on the Heidelberg Catechism* (Phillipsburg, New Jersey: 1994).

SECONDARY SOURCES

1700s
Bayle, Pierre. *Dictionnaire Historique et Critique*. Tome 1. (Paris: P. Brunel, 1730).
Kelham, Robert. *Dictionary of the Norman or Old French Language*. (London: Edward Brook 1779).

1800s
Baird, Henry Martyn. *History of the Rise of the Huguenots*, 2 vols. (London: Hodder and Stoughton, 1880).
Brette, Ernest. *Du Système de Moïse Amyraut Désigné Sous le Nom d'Universalisme Hypothétique: Thèse Publiquement Soutenue à la Faculté de Théologie Protestante de Montauban en Juillet 1855*. (Montauban: Forestié Neveu et Cie, 1855).
Lee, Hannah F. *The Huguenots in France and America*. (Cambridge, MA: Clearfield, 1843).
Roehrich, T.E. *La Doctrine De La Prédestination Et L'école De Saumur: Thèse Soutenue du Faculté de Théologie Protestante de Strasbourg*. (Strasbourg, Heitz, 1867).
Sabatier, André. *Étude historique sur l'universalisme hypothétique de Moïse Amyraut: Thèse Soutenue à la Faculté de Théologie de Montauban*. (Toulouse: Chauvin, 1867).
Saigey, Charles Edmond. *Moïse Amyraut: Sa vie et Ses Écrits*. (Strasbourg: l'Académie, 1849).
Viguié, A. "Amyraut" In *Encyclopédie des Sciences Réligieuses*, vol. 1, 273–85. (Paris: Sandoz and Fischbacher, 1877).

1900s and after
Allen, David L. and Steve W. Lemke, eds. *Whosoever Will: A Biblical-Theological Critique of Five Point Calvinism*. (Nashville: B & H, 2010).
Armstrong, Brian G. *Calvinism and the Amyraut Heresy*. (Madison: University of Wisconsin Press, 1969).

Barnes, Tom. *Atonement Matters: A Call to Declare the Biblical View of the Atonement.* (Webster, NY: Evangelical Press, 2008).
Beilby, James and Paul R. Eddy, eds. *The Nature of the Atonement: Four Views.* Downers Grove: IVP, 2006).
Beik, William. *A Social and Cultural History of Early Modern France.* (Cambridge: Cambridge University Press, 2009).
Benedict, Philip. *The Faith and Fortunes of France's Huguenots, 1600–85.* (Burlington, VT: Ashgate, 2001).
_____. *Christ's Churches Purely Reformed.* (New Haven: Yale University Press, 2002).
_____, ed. *Cities and Social Change in Early Modern France.* (New York, Routledge, 1992).
Boersma, Hans. *A Hot Peppercorn: Richard Baxter's Doctrine of Justification in Its Seventeenth-Century Context of Controversy.* (Zoetermeer: Uitgeverij Boekencentrum, 1993).
Briggs, Robin. *Early Modern France: 1560–1715.* (Oxford: Oxford University Press, 1989).
Clifford, A.C. *Atonement and Justification: English Evangelical Theology 1640–1790: An Evaluation.* (Oxford: Clarendon Press, 1990).
_____. *Calvinus: Authentic Calvinism: A Clarification.* (Norwich: Charenton: Reformed Publishing, 1996).
_____. *Amyraut Affirmed.* (Norwich: Charenton, 2004).
Cottret, Bernard. "Calvin, Etait-Il Calviniste?" *Bulletin Du Centre Protestant D'Etudes* 7 (November, 2009): 4–18.
Dever, Mark and Michael Lawrence, eds. *It is Well: Expositions on Substitutionary Atonement.* Wheaton: Crossway, 2010).
De Jong, J. Editor. *Crisis in the Reformed Churches.* (Grand Rapids: Reformed Fellowship, 1968).
Douty, Norman F. *The Death of Christ; A Treatise Which Answers the Question: "Did Christ Die Only for the Elect?"* (Swengel, PA: Reiner Publications, 1972).
_____. *Did Christ Die Only For the Elect? A Treatise On The Extent Of the Atonement.* (Eugene, OR: Wipf & Stock Publishers, 1998).
Fesko, John Valero. *Diversity Within the Reformed Tradition: Supra- and Infralapsarianism in Calvin, Dort and Westminister.* (Jackson, MS: Reformed Academic Press, 1999).

Gamble, Richard, ed., *An Elaboration of the Theology of John Calvin*, vol. 8, (New York: Garland Publishing, 1992).

Gibson, David and Jonathan Gibson, eds., *From Heaven He Came and Sought Her: Definite Atonement in Historical, Biblical, Theological, and Pastoral Perspective*. (Wheaton, IL: Crossway, 2013).

Fluhrer, Gabriel, ed. *Atonement*. (Phillipsburg, NJ: P & R Publishing, 2010).

Hall, Basil, "Calvin against the Calvinists," in *John Calvin* (Grand Rapids: Eerdmans, 1966), 19-37.

Helm, Paul. *Calvin and the Calvinists*. (Edinburgh: The Banner of Truth, 1982).

Hill, Charles, E. and Frank A. James III, eds. *The Glory of the Atonement: Biblical, Theological, and Practical Perspectives*. (Downers Grove, IL, IVP, 2004).

Hindley, Alan; Frederick Langley and Brian Levy, eds., *Old French-English Dictionary*. (Cambridge: Cambridge University Press, 2000.

Holt, Mack P. *The French Wars of Religion: 1562-1629*. (Cambridge: Cambridge University Press, 2005).

Johnson, William, S. and John H. Leith, Editors. *Reformed Reader*. Vol. 1. (Louisville: Westminster John Knox, 1993).

Kendall, R.T. *Calvin and English Calvinism to 1649*. (UK: Paternoster Press, 1997).

Kennedy, Kevin. *Union with Christ and the Extent of the Atonement*. (Bern: Peter Lang, 2002).

Kertzer, David I. and Marzio Barbagli, eds., *Family Life in Early Modern Times: 1500-1789*. (New Haven: Yale University Press, 2001).

Knecht, Robert J. *The French Religious Wars: 1562-1598*. (Oxford: Osprey, 2002).

Kuiper, Rienk, B. *For Whom Did Christ Die? A Study of the Divine Design of the Atonement*. (Eugene, OR: Wipf & Stock Publishers, 1993).

Kuiper, Herman. *Calvin on Common Grace*. (Grand Rapids: Baker, 1928).

La Planche, Francois. *Orthodoxie et Prédication: l'Œuvre d'Amyraut et la Querelle de la Grace Universelle*. (Paris: Presses Universitaires de France, 1965).

Lightner, Robert Paul. *The Death Christ Died; A Case for Unlimited Atonement*. (Des Plaines, IL, Regular Baptist Press, 1967).

Long, Gary, D. *Definite Atonement*. (Frederick, MD: New Covenant Media, 2006).

Mentzer, Raymond A. and Andrew Spicer, eds., *Society and Culture in the Huguenot World: 1559-1685*. (Cambridge: Cambridge University Press, 2002).

Méteyer, Louis-Jules. *L'Académie Protestante de Saumur*, (rev. ed. Paris: La Cause, 2005).

Moore, Jonathan. *English Hypothetical Universalism: John Preston and the Softening of Reformed Theology*. (Grand Rapids: Eerdmans, 2007).
Muller, Richard, A. *After Calvin: Studies in the Development of a Theological Tradition*. (Oxford: Oxford University Press, 2003).
_____. *Calvin and the Reformed Tradition: On the Work of Christ and the Order of Salvation*. (Grand Rapids: Baker, 2012).
_____. *Christ and Decree*. (Grand Rapids: Baker, 1988).
_____. *Post-Reformation Reformed Dogmatics: The Rise and Development of Reformed Orthodoxy, ca. 1520 to ca. 1725*. Four volumes. (Grand Rapids: Baker Academic, 2003).
_____. *The Unaccomodated Calvin*. (New York: OUP, 2000).
_____. *Christ and the Decree: Christology and Predestination in Reformed Theology from Calvin to Perkins*. (Durham: Labyrinth Press, 1986).
Murray, John. *For Whom Did Christ Die?: The Extent of the Atonement*. (Birmingham: Solid Ground Christian Books, 2010).
Nicole, Roger. "Covenant, Universal Call, and Definite Atonement," in *Standing Forth*. (Geanies-House, UK: Mentor, 2002).
_____. *Moyse Amyraut: A Bibliography with Special Reference to the Controversy on Universal Grace*. (New York: Garland Publishing, 1981).
Packer, J.I. and Mark Dever. *In My Place Condemned He Stood: Celebrating the Glory of the Atonement*. (Wheaton: Crossway, 2007).
Peterson, Robert, A. *Calvin and The Atonement*. (Geanies House, Scotland: Mentor, 2009).
Potter, David. *A History of France: 1460–1560*. (New York: St. Martin, 1995).
Rainbow, J.H. *The Will of God and The Cross*. (Pennsylvania: Pickwick Publications, 1990).
Rickard, Peter. *The French Language in the Seventeenth Century*. (Woodbridge, Suffolk: D. S. Brewer, 1992).
Rohls, Jan. *Reformed Confessions: Theology from Zurich to Barmen*. (Louisville: Westminster John Knox, 1987).
Smiles, Samuel. *The Huguenots in France*. (London: Routledge & Sons, 1903).
Stauffer, Richard. *Moise Amyraut: Un Precurseur Français De L'OEcumenisme*. (Paris: Cahors, 1962).
_____. *The Quest For Church Unity: From John Calvin to Isaac d'Huisseau*. (Allison Park, PA: Pickwick Publications, 1986).
Strehle, Stephan. *Calvinism, Federalism, and Scholasticism: A Study of the Reformed Doctrine of Covenant*. (Bern: Peter Lang, 1988).

Thomas, Michael G. *The Extent of the Atonement : A Dilemma for Reformed Theology from Calvin to the Consensus (1536–1675)*. Studies in Christian History and Thought. (Eugene, OR: Wipf & Stock Publishers, 2007).
Trueman, Carl. *The Claims of Truth: John Owen's Trinitarian Theology*. Cumbria: Paternoster Press, 1998).
_____. *Histories and Fallacies*. Wheaton, IL: Crossway, 2010).
Trueman, Carl and R. Scott Clark, eds., *Protestant Scholasticism: Essays in Reassessment*. Carlisle: Paternoster, 1999).
Van Stam, F.P. *The Controversy Over the Theology of Saumur (1635–1650): Disrupting the Debates Among Huguenots in Complicated Circumstances*. Amsterdam: Holland University Press, 1988).
Vickers, Brian. *Jesus' Blood and Righteousness: Paul's Theology of Imputation*. Wheaton: Crossway, 2006).

PERIODICALS

Bell, M. Charles. "Calvin and the Extent of the Atonement." *The Evangelical Quarterly* 55 (1983): 115–123.
Cook, Peter. "Calvin and the Atonement." A Review in *Evangelical Quarterly* 74, no. 3 (2002): 279.
De Lima, Leandro Antonio. "Calvino Ensinou a Expiação Limitada?" *Fides Reformata* 9, no. 1 (2004): 77–99.
Fleyfel, Antoine. "Les Aspects Désacralisants De La Théologie De Moyse Amyraut." *Etudes Théologiques et Réligieuses* 85, no. 1 (2010): 45–59.
Gerrish, B. A. "Union with Christ and the Extent of the Atonement in Calvin." A Review in *Theology Today* 61, no. 1 (2004): 142–144.
Gomes, Alan W. "Faustus Socinus and John Calvin on the Merits of Christ." *Reformation & Renaissance Review: Journal of the Society for Reformation Studies* 12, no. 2/3 (2010): 189–205.
Gunton, Colin. "Aspects of Salvation: Some Unscholastic Themes from Calvin's Institutes." *International Journal of Systematic Theology* 1, no. 3 (1999): 253.
Karlberg, Mark W., "The Extent of the atonement: A Dilemma for Reformed Theology from Calvin to the Consensus (1536–1675)", *Trinity Journal*, 04 (1999): 116.
Klauber, Martin I. "The Helvetic Formula Consensus (1675): An Introduction and Translation." *Trinity Journal* 11, no. 1 (1990): 103–123.

Kleinman, Ruth. "Calvinismus Und Franzosische Monarchie Im 17. Jahrhundert." *American Historical Review* 82, no. 4 (1977): 977.

Lewis, Stephen. "Moise Amyraut 1596–1664: Predestination and the Atonement Debate." *Chafer Theological Seminary Journal*, 1, no. 3 (Winter 1995): 4–11.

Macleod, Donald. "Amyraldus Redivivus: A Review Article." *Evangelical Quarterly* 81, no. 3 (2009): 210–229.

McGowan, A. T. B. "Amyraldianism—Is It Modified Calvinism?/Amyraut Affirmed." *Evangelical Quarterly* 77, no. 2 (2005): 186–187.

Moltmann, Jurgen. "Pradestination und Heilsgeschichte bei Moyse Amyraut," *Zeitschrift Fur Kirchengeschichte* 65 (1954): 270–303.

Moore, Jonathan D. "Calvin Versus the Calvinists? The Case of John Preston (1587–1628)." *Reformation & Renaissance Review: Journal of the Society for Reformation Studies* 6, no. 3 (2004): 327–348.

Nicole, Roger. "John Calvin's View of the Extent of the Atonement." *Westminster Theological Journal* 47, no. 2 (Fall 1985): 197–225.

Placher, William C., John Flett, Michael Purcell, Lain Taylor, Andrew T. Lincoln, Paul M. Collins, W. Ross Hastings, and Nathan R. Strunk. "Reviews." *International Journal of Systematic Theology* 7, no. 3 (2005): 316–342.

Rouwendal, P. L. "Calvin's Forgotten Classical Position on the Extent of the Atonement: About Sufficiency, Efficiency, and Anachronism." *Westminster Theological Journal*, Fall (2008): 317–335.

Strehle, Stephen. "The Extent of the Atonement and the Synod of Dort." *Westminster Theological Journal* 51, no. 1 (1989): 1–23.

̶̶̶̶. "Universal Grace and Amyraldianism." *Westminster Theological Journal* 51, no. 2 (1989): 345–357.

Veldman, Meine. "Secrets of Moltmann's Tacit Tradition: Via Covenant Theology to Promise Theology." *Journal of Reformed Theology* 4, no. 3 (2010): 208–239.

Wallace, Peter, J. "The Doctrine of the Covenant in the Elenctic Theology of Francis Turretin," *Mid-America Journal of Theology*, 13 (2002): 143–179.

Witt, Jared L. "Union with Christ and the Extent of the Atonement in Calvin." A Review in *Renaissance Quarterly* 58, no. 2 (2005): 626–628.

Wright, Nigel G. "Predestination and Perseverance in the Early Theology of Jürgen Moltmann." *Evangelical Quarterly* 83, no. 4 (2011): 330–345.

Dissertations

Archibald, Paul N. "A Comparative Study of John Calvin and Theodore Beza on the Doctrine of the Extent of the Atonement." Ph.D. diss. (Westminster Theological Seminary, 1998).

Beardslee, John W. "Theological Developments at Geneva under Francis and Jean-Alphonse Turretin (1648–1737)." Ph.D. Diss. (Yale University, 1956).

Berry, H.E. "The Amyraldian Controversy an its Implications for the Lutheran-Reformed Unity in the Doctrine of Grace." B.D. thesis (Concordia Theological Seminary, 1970).

Chambers, N.A. "A Critical Examination of John Owen's Argument for Limited Atonement in the Death of Death in the Death of Christ," Th.M. thesis (Reformed Theological Seminary, 1998).

Daniel, C. "Hyper-Calvinism and John Gill." Ph.D. diss. (University of Edinburgh, 1983).

Godfrey, W.R. "Tensions Within International Calvinism: The Debate on the Atonement at the Synod of Dort, 1618–1619." Ph.D. diss. (Stanford University, 1974).

Gootjes, Albert J. "Claude Pajon (1626–1685) and the Academy of Saumur." PhD. Diss. (Calvin College, 2012).

Grohman, D.D. "The Genevan Reactions to the Saumur Doctrine of Hypothetical Universalism, 1635–1685." Th.D. diss. (Knox College in cooperation with Toronto School of Theology, 1971).

Harmon, Matthew Paul, "Moyse Amyraut's Six Sermons: Directions for Amyrauldian Studies." Th.M. thesis (Westminster Theological Seminary, 2008).

Jensen, Paul T. "Calvin and Turretin: A Comparison of their Soteriologies." Ph.D. diss. (University of Virginia, 1988).

Moltmann, Jurgen. "Gnadenbund und Gnadenwahl: Die Praedestinationslehredes Moyse Amyraut, dargestellt im Zusammenhang der heilsgeschichtlich-foederaltheologie Tradition der Akademie von Saumur." Ph.D. diss. (Göttingen, 1951).

Nicole, R. "Moyse Amyraut (1596–1664) and the Controversy on Universal Grace: First Phase (1634–1637)." Ph.D. diss. (Harvard University, 1966).

Nomura, S. "The Extent of the Atonement in Calvin's Concept of the Preaching of the Gospel." Th.M. thesis (Western Theological Seminary, 1991).

Proctor, L. "The Theology of Moïse Amyraut Considered as a Reaction Against Seventeenth-Century Calvinism." Ph.D. diss. (University of Leeds, 1952).

Shultz, Gary L. "A Biblical and Theological Defense of a Multi-Intentioned View of the Atonement." Ph.D. diss. (Southern Baptist Theologican Seminary, 2008).

Wenkel, David, "John Bunyan's Theory of Atonement in His Early Doctrinal and Polemic Works Amyraldian or Particular?" M.A. thesis (Trinity Evangelical Divinity School, 2004).

Index of Scripture

Genesis

1:26	70
2:7	78
3:6	74
3:15	100
3:17	88
3:23–24	87
6:5, 8	89
45:7–8	76

Exodus

9:12–16	76
23:3	122

1 Samuel

2:25	76

2 Samuel

12:11–12	76
16:10	76

Job

14:4	89

Psalms

1:6	115
8:3–6	71
19:1-2	64
51:7	89
115:3	60
145:9	66

Proverbs

1:22	138
24:21	25

Ezekiel

36:26	109

Matthew

22:14	115

John

1:12	97
3:5	109
3:14-16	106
3:16	104
3:36	106
6:35, 40	105
6:40	97

6:44	109
6:45	110, 133
8:44	75
14:6	102
14:9	96
17:3	132
17:9	157
17:11, 15–17, 20–21	157

Acts

4:12	102
4:27–28	76
4:28	60
5:29	24
10:34	101
13:46-47	101
13:48	167
15	32

Romans

1:14	101
1:19-20	69
1:19–20	103
1:91-20	111
2:4	102
5:3–11	158
5:12	71, 87, 89
5:18	19
6:4	93
6:16-17	85
6:20	108
6:23	89
8:3	94
8:7	109
8:11	97
8:16	97
8:17	97
8:20	88
8:28	109
8:28-39	159
8:29	60, 96, 114, 144
8:29-30	60
9:10-12	118
9:14	119
9:15	156
9:18	116
9:19	116
9:20-21	116
10:18	111
11:2	115
11:23	109
11:33	120
12:2	140
14:23	117

1 Corinthians

1:2	93
1:21	168
1:30	94
2:4	133
2:8	141
2:9	94, 155
15:42–54	79
15:45	78
15:47-49	96
15:47–55	80

2 Corinthians

2:18	152
3:18	152
4:4	139
11:3	74

Galatians

4:8-9	115
6:10	33

Ephesians

1:4–5	157
1:5	60
1:11	60
1:17	138
1:17-18	110
1:17-19	132
1:19-20	133
2:1	109
2:1, 3	89
2:4-5	114
2:5, 10	109
2:6-7	117
3:18-19	133
4:3	140
4:24	93

Philippians

2:13	109
3:21	96
4:7	141

Colossians

1:13	109

2 Thessalonians

3:2	118

1 Timothy

2:4	106

3:1–14	31
4:5-6	103
5:17	32

2 Timothy

1:9	118
2:19	128

Titus

1:1	118
1:5–7	31
2:11	103
2:11-14	94
3:5	140

Hebrews

1:3	96
11:6	117

1 Peter

1:2	141
1:20	115
2:17	24, 25, 27
3:11	48
5:3	32

2 Peter

1:4	97

1 John

1:6	139
2:2	103
2:9-11	149
3:2	94

3:8   93
3:9   97
4:7   97
5:9-10   106

Index of Names

A

Amyraldus. *See* Amyraut, Moses
Amyraut, Mme   33
Amyraut, Moses   7, 8, 9, 11, 12,
    13, 15, 16, 17, 18, 19, 20, 21, 22,
    23, 24, 25, 26, 27, 28, 29, 30, 31,
    32, 33, 34, 35, 41, 42, 43, 44, 45,
    46, 47, 48, 49, 50, 163, 164, 165,
    166, 167, 168, 169
Aristotle   16
Arminius, Jakob   19
Armstrong, Brian G.   15, 21, 44, 50
Audebert, Father   20
Aymon, Jean   15

B

Baird, Henry   13
Baxter, Richard   12, 36
Bayle, Pierre   16, 18
Bedford, Duke of. *See* Russell, William
Benedict, Philip   19
Beza, Theodore   16, 19, 20, 31
le Blanc, Stephen (pastor and professor in the Academy of Die)   165
de Bons, Amédéé (pastor in the Church of Chalons upon Saône)   165

du Bosc, Pierre   35
Bouchereau, M.   16

C

Calamy, Edmund   14
Calvin, John   11, 16, 18, 19, 20, 21, 22, 24, 25, 28, 31
Cameron, John   16
Capell, Louis   17
de Caumont, Armand-Nompar, Duke de la Forc   30
Charles I. *See* Stuart, Charles I, King of Great Britain
Charles II. *See* Stuart, Charles I, King of Great Britain
Charles, Pierre (pastor in the Church of Montauban)   164
Cicero, Marcus Tullius. *See* Tully
Clifford, Alan C.   50, 99
Commarc, Jean (pastor in the Church of Verteuil)   164
de Comminges, Gaston, Count of Comminges   28
Condé, Duke of   26
Cousins (or Cosin), John, Bishop of Durham   31

D

Daillé, Adrien 28
Daillé, Jean 17, 28, 30, 32, 33, 165
Davenant, John 21
de L'Angle, Jean-Maximilien (pastor in the Church of Rouen) 164
Demosthenes 16

E

Evans, John 14

F

le Faucheur, Michel (pastor in the Church of Paris) 164
Flavel, John 13

G

Garnier, Isaac (pastor of the Church of Marchenoir) 164
Giles, Daniel 41
Gomarus, Francis 16
Guilaut, Count of 28

H

Hale, Sir Matthew 13
Harcourt, Count 26
Heath, Richard 13
Henri IV, King of France 17
Henry, Matthew 14
Hervart, M. 23, 30
Hoard, Samuel 21
Hutton, Hugh 15

I

Innocent XI, Pope. *See* Odescalchi, Benedetto

J

Jeffreys, George, 1st Baron Jeffreys of Wem, Judge 12

L

Lederer, Marianne 41
Louis XIII, King of France 18, 26
Louis XIV, King of France 26, 31, 35
Lum, Richard 50

M

Mazarin, Jules Raymond, Cardinal-Duke of Rethel, Mayenne and Nevers 26, 27, 30
Moulin, Pierre du 18, 164
Muller, Richard 19

N

Nicole, Roger 19

O

Odescalchi, Benedetto (Pope Innocent XI) 15
Ouzan, Sieur (elder in the Church of Saumur) 164
Owen, John 18

P

de Péréfixe, Paul Philippe Hardouin de
    Beaumont, Archbishop of Paris
        32
Petit, Samuel (pastor and professor in
    the Church and Academy of
    Nîmes)   165
de la Place, Josué   17, 22, 163
du Plessis, Armand-Jean, Cardinal
    Richelieu, Duke of Richelieu
    and of Fronsac   18, 20, 25, 26
Plessis-Mornay, Lord Philippe du 16, 28

Q

Quick, John   12, 13, 14, 15, 23, 26, 29, 31, 34, 35

R

Richelieu, Cardinal. *See* du Plessis, Armand-Jean
Rickard, Peter   44
Rivet, André, (pastor and
    Professor at Leyden)   164
Russell, William, Duke of Bedford   15

S

Smiles, Samuel   13
Stam, Frans Pieter van   15, 19
Stuart, Charles II, King of
    Great Britain   14
Stuart, Charles I, King of
    Great Britain   25

T

Testard, Paul, of Blois 20, 163, 164, 165, 166, 167, 168, 169
Tully   16
Turenne, Charlotte, Princess of Tarente   30

V

Vignier, Nicholas (pastor in the
    Church of Blois)   164
de Villarnoul, Lord   28
Villeneuve, M.   20
Vinay, J   41

W

Ward, Seth, Bishop of Exeter   13

The Translator

Besides studying at various academic institutions in the United States since the 1990s, Dr Matthew Scott Harding (b. 1973) has also pursued post-doctoral studies on this side of the Atlantic: at Université De Genève from 2010–13 (Reformation Theology) and Regents Park, Oxford University in 2012 (British Reformation). Utilizing his wide-ranging linguistic skills (Hebrew, Greek, French and German), the present work originated as his Ph.D. dissertation: 'A Critical Analysis of Moïse Amyraut's Atonement Theory Based on a New and Critical Translation of a *Brief Treatise on Predestination* (Southwestern Baptist Theological Seminary, 2014). Author of several articles and papers, Dr Harding's varied activities have extended his ministry to India and China. A member of several professional societies (including the Sixteenth Century Society, the American Society of Church History, the American Academy of Religion and the Calvin Studies Society), he currently combines a guest lectureship at Dallas Theological Seminary with serving as the Lead Pastor of The WELL Community Church, Argyle, Texas. Married to Jennifer, Dr and Mrs Harding have a daughter, Sarai and a son, Jonathan.

The Biographer

Dr Alan C. Clifford (b. 1941) has been interested in Amyraldian theology for many years. His convictions emerged during his doctoral research, an in-depth study of Arminianism and Calvinism. His thesis *Atonement and Justification* was published by Oxford University Press in 1990. Author of several books, articles and papers (and a few hymns) on this and related themes (including biographies of Philip Doddridge, John Calvin & the Huguenots, and the Welsh Calvinistic Methodist preacher John Jones, Talsarn), Dr Clifford has been absorbed in Baxter studies in recent years. His latest book *Richard Baxter: The Gospel Truth* (Charenton Reformed Publishing, 2016) is a detailed vindication of the 'authentic Calvinism' affirmed by both Amyraut and Baxter. Married to Marian (with a grown-up family), Dr Clifford is currently Pastor of Norwich Reformed Church.